The

Do-it-Yourself Therapy Book for Depression

Inspiring, Insightful,
and Practical Guide
for a Better Mood
and Freedom from Anxiety

ROSE C. MANALO

author of
Depression and Intense Anxieties:
Your Quickest Way Out

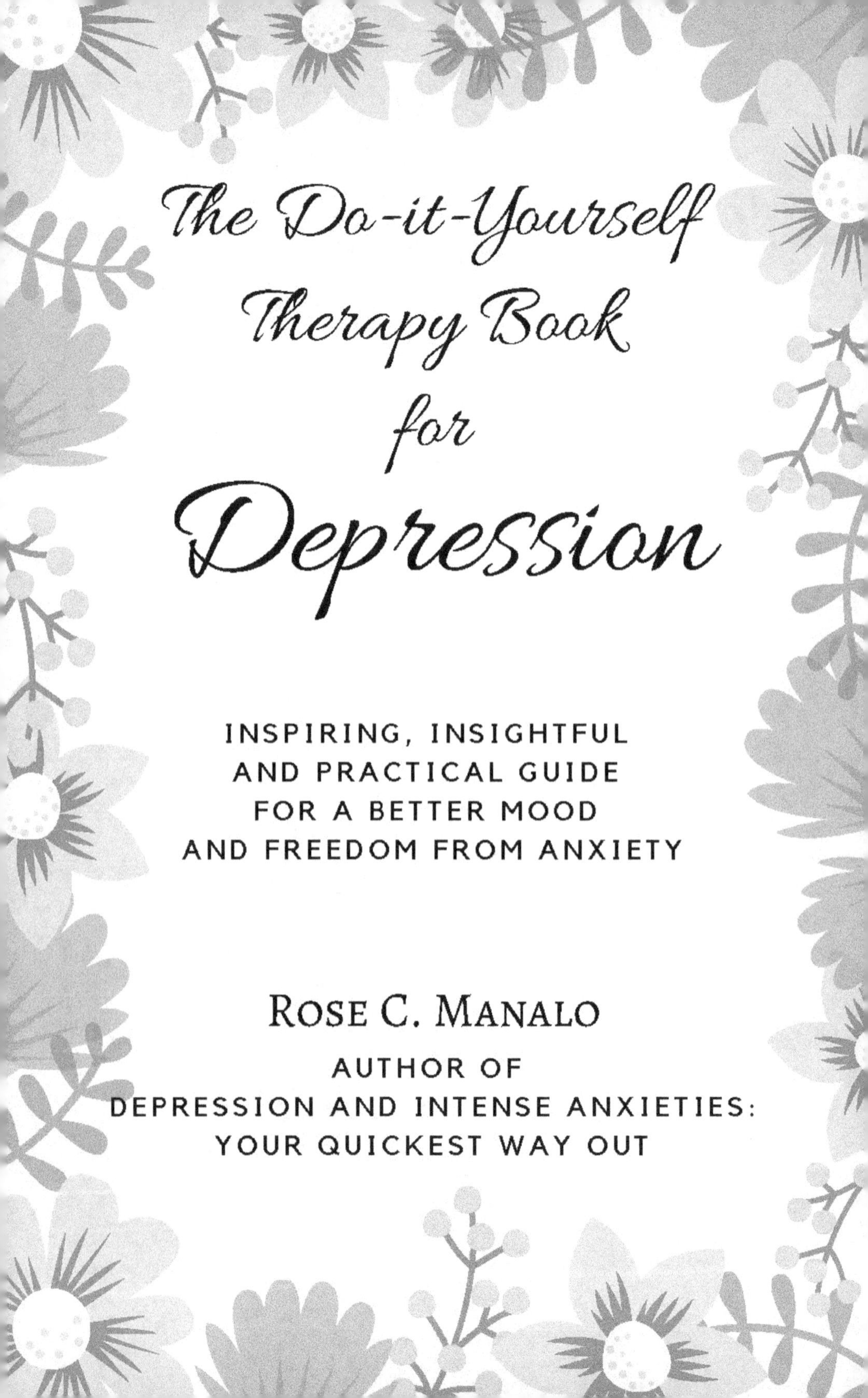

The Do-it-Yourself Therapy Book

for

Depression

INSPIRING, INSIGHTFUL
AND PRACTICAL GUIDE
FOR A BETTER MOOD
AND FREEDOM FROM ANXIETY

ROSE C. MANALO

AUTHOR OF
DEPRESSION AND INTENSE ANXIETIES:
YOUR QUICKEST WAY OUT

The Do-it-Yourself
Therapy Book for
Depression
By Rose C. Manalo
Published by Neverbound Publishing House
74 Bel Air Drive, Cor. Fremont St., Laguna Bel Air 1, Don Jose,
Sta. Rosa City, Laguna, Region 4-A, Philippines
Twitter @rosecmanalo1
Instagram @rosecmanalo1
Facebook www.facebook.com/rosecmanalo1
Email rosalinamanalo1970@yahoo.com

Medical Disclaimer:
All information, content, and material in this book is for informational
purposes only and are not intended to serve as a substitute for the
consultation, diagnosis, and/or medical treatment of a qualified physician
or healthcare provider.

ISBN
Softbound/Paperback: 978-621-8153-08-0
Hardbound: 978-621-8153-07-3
E-Book: 978-621-8153-11-0

Contents

Preface

The physical manifestations of depression and intense anxieties started to show one twilight morning, in January 2008, while I was driving home. All of a sudden, the steering wheel seemed too thin. I tried to grab it harder, but my fingers couldn't stay tight around it. I had to lean forward so I could press it with my elbows to keep it steady. However, doing so made me faint from being out of breath despite my heavy and rapid breathing. Air, as with strength, seem to have disappeared.

Realizing I was losing control of these basic faculties, my heart raced even faster. Soon my knees felt weak as well. I thought… should I pull over at the next gas station? No, I can't, because that would require maneuverings to get across 3 lanes. I repeatedly swallowed hard. My mouth tasted sour and my cheeks burned with acid. The motorists behind me started honking. I knew I was moving too slow, but I couldn't do anything about it. My hand shook as I reached out to press the hazard button and began my slide to the outermost lane. I had thought I was still at least 15 minutes away from the exit, but it unexpectedly appeared as soon as I entered the outermost lane. I realized I was driving mindlessly most of the time.

Enveloped by God's divine protection, I got home safely. Surely, I thought, being home would make all these terrible symptoms subside? I was wrong. They stayed and persisted for three horrifying years. The first 6 months were the most debilitating. I barely managed to get 3 hours of sleep each night as I was constantly awoken by my pounding heartbeats. No matter how hard I tried, I couldn't sleep past 2 a.m. Those last 4 hours before dawn were the most difficult part of the day into which my mind was ushered by overpowering sense of forebodings that led to floods of negative and hopeless thoughts which played in constant loops in my head.

Each long loop of negative thoughts would start with painful recollections of the details surrounding our recently failed bakery franchised business and its consequences. Aggressive thoughts of blame raced in my mind and filled me up with rage and desire for revenge. Those vindictive thoughts would then alternate with even more crippling self-blaming thoughts. A lot of "what-if" and "why" questions bounced obstinately in my head, each one failing to offer any relief from the torture of self-blame.

All this mental agony left me weak in my limbs. My knees felt like jelly and I walked close to the walls while holding on to furniture for support. I had to constantly breathe deeply to get in enough air. The pounding chest palpitations continued through the day and seemed to intensify at night when it was quieter, and these palpitations were all I heard. On the second month, as if my sufferings weren't enough, I started feeling a constant sharp pain in my chest that seemed like the tip of a knife was stuck in my chest.

Each night I hoped that I would wake up the next day free from this dreadful condition. But each morning proved to be an unanswered prayer. Being a Christian who firmly believed in the redemptive power of Jesus Christ on the Cross, experiencing these tormenting manifestations of depression, profoundly confused me. But that's all it could do to my faith. All depression could manage was to make me ask "how could I have this much faith in God and feel this bad at the same time?". It means that my faith in my eternal salvation was never shaken. But my physical being was not mirroring this faith. And this must be why the Apostle John, in his 3rd epistle, 3 John 2 gave us the warning to make sure "that our physical body is as healthy as our soul and spirit is healthy". After all, I was made of spirit and soul, living temporarily in this physical body.

My physical body, through depression, was screaming for help. It was sending signals that it was severely depleted from the recent stresses that it had gone through. It needed replenishment. It needed repair. It was very inflamed, and it needed to heal. My body was literally in the PIT STOP of depression. A pit stop of extreme importance.

In my first book, *Depression and Intense Anxieties: Your Quickest Way Out*, I wrote exhaustively how I healed from depression by "giving in" to my body's true cravings. It started on the day I exposed my skin to the blazing morning sun, without any sun lotion on. The immediate lift in my mood and the physical strength that started to seep in within minutes of being exposed to sunshine, confirmed my growing suspicions that, indeed, my body was missing a lot of things. More confirmations followed along with steady healing as I gave in and indulged on the nutrients that my body craved for. Please do take the time to read this first book.

In this second book, while my physical being was undergoing healing, I reveal how my mental and emotional faculties were attempting to realign themselves and heal as well. I wrote about how, if we are just willing enough to effect changes in these areas presenting themselves ripe for improvement, that we can emerge from depression with our life's purpose in hand. Depression is your own season for change. If we can just see it for what it is, depression can be the catapult that can shoot you forward like no other life experience can.

Introduction

Each Therapy Chapter has three parts:

Prose, Poetry and Meditations.

Prose

While it is unlikely that two persons suffering from depression have the same exact triggers, we cannot deny that we've all had the same bitter taste of this dreadful "mental" condition: the constant terrifying sense of foreboding and hopelessness, that perpetual queasy sensation in the gut, the weakness in the limbs, the persistent mental pull to focus on the negative things, the inability to get satisfaction from sleep, and the constant need to breathe deeply as an attempt to ease our chests from the burden of unrelenting pounding palpitations. These and many other harrowing characteristics of depression, in different shades of severity, are the common grounds shared by most people who suffer from it.

In this part of each therapy chapter, you will witness how each of these awful facets of depression was dealt with and whether there was success or not. You will have an unobstructed view of the nitty gritty, the darkest and most naked of thoughts, the smallest and biggest of steps taken, and all the failures and successes in between. You will see how seemingly insignificant steps can prove to be reliable lifeline out of your horrible pit of depression. From these intimate efforts, you can draw out your own customized templates for therapy that you can readily use any given time that you need them, anywhere, unlimited times, for free.

It is my hope that you would find the same courage that I had that enabled me to strip my mind naked as I faced the only person in the Therapy Room: ME. Once you realized that you can face and look in the eye this stark-naked person that you are - that you are willing to improve the areas that you can and accept those you cannot - then you have the rest of the therapy time to enjoy.

Poetry

*S*o many of my experiences with depression aren't easy to express in a regular manner, without feeling obliged to make sure things aren't misunderstood. Hence, the poems are the rest and crudest of thoughts I couldn't convey through prose. Using poetry as a means to bring out the deepest recesses of my soul affords me a certain tolerance where I don't feel the usual need to justify or explain. It is depression in its rawest form.

However, I did take advantage of the facilities of metrics and rhyme to tone down emotions like anger, grief and shame and make them inviting enough to look at.

If you haven't, I encourage you to try poetry as another means of therapy. It's liberating and nonjudgmental.

Meditations

*m*any are missing out on the Bible's supreme ability to transform lives. It is often regarded as being impractical and its principles too impossible for daily application. The total opposite is what the Bible is. It is God's perfect design for mankind's time on earth. Both practical and doable, the principles it teaches override any geographical, social, religious and racial differences.

My meditations on this God-breathed book, highlighted by my experience with severe depression, made me realize that indeed, I was created for a beautiful purpose. The God who created me was intentional and mindful of how He designed me and the purposes for which He made that design. The main proof that this is so are the talents that I knew I had since I was a young girl. These talents that He bestowed on me were indications of His intended purpose for my life. However, the

Word of God is the combined vital compass and rudder that could steer me to the best route to take to achieve my life's purpose.

Unfortunately, at the time that I could have benefitted from its wisdom the most, I didn't make use of the Word as an efficient steering mechanism. Instead, I chose diverging roads that seemed to offer quicker, wider, shorter and with the least obstructions visible. They proved to be very poor choices. Those bad decisions led to consequences that opened the gates of incredible stresses. In a very short period of time, I collapsed under the weight of these stresses and tumbled inside the all-too-wide door of severe depression.

The Holy Scriptures is for anyone who wants to live a purposeful life on earth and seeks the least painful route to have it.

But it is also for anyone who is right in the middle of depression, wants to find their way out and eager to understand all the whys of their having depression.

Understanding all those reasons, through the guidance of the Word of God, and keeping your physical body healthy, these are what will keep you from sliding back into depression.

Chapter 1: Kick out the gate-crashers

During my depressed years, the busiest part of me, next to my heart, was my mind. There was always something going on in my mind. One day I was hunched over the washing machine, without realizing it had stopped moving. My mind was busy thinking about a woman I talked to recently and the things that she had told me. I felt my eyebrows and my eyes were suddenly painful from frowning. I realized that my thoughts had gone way beyond what had actually taken place. I was recalling things that never happened and words that the person never said. I remember furiously shaking my head and closing my eyes, then in my mind I did an about-face, and confronted myself, *"Rose, those things never happened. That person never said those words. Stop imagining things. Stick to facts."*

That wasn't the first time that I had let my thoughts go wild, but that was the very first time that I acknowledged what I was doing and opposed myself. And I was surprised at what "I" did. **"I" shut up**. The inner me suddenly stopped thinking, talking, and imagining things. Now that I was aware of what I have been thinking and how my mind was concocting things that never happened, I felt too ashamed of doing more of those. How could I have let imaginary things deplete whatever little energy I had left? What foolishness it was to feel too anxious and even hurt by things that never took place? Didn't I have enough going on already that I had to imagine things that added to my anxieties?

That was the day I realized that, yes, I may not have complete control over what enters my mind, but, I do have complete control over what stays and lingers. That was the start of the end of my "zombie" days. It was not automatic though. I had to learn to really want to be in control of my mind. And at times I had to sift through my thoughts and identify the real guests from the gate-crashers. I had to learn to appreciate realities over make-believe.

Practical Guide:

The moment that you sense a shift in your mood, feelings, or even facial expressions, make an about-face and analyze what you have been thinking for the last few minutes. The key is to be honest to yourself as you sift through your thoughts. Use Philippians 4:8 as your mental sieve.

No matter how tempting it is to keep them, **kick out the gate-crashers!**

I Rule

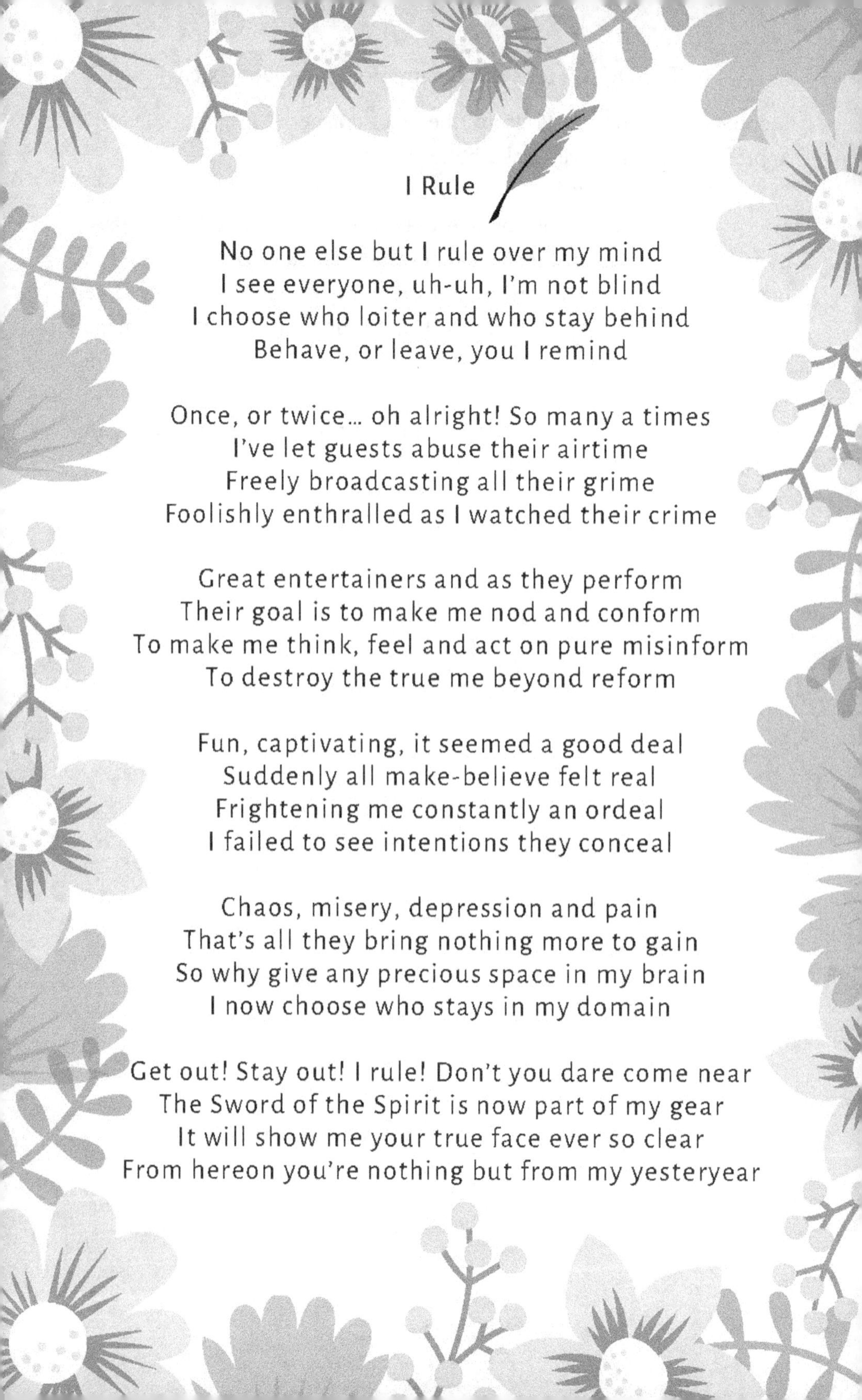

No one else but I rule over my mind
I see everyone, uh-uh, I'm not blind
I choose who loiter and who stay behind
Behave, or leave, you I remind

Once, or twice… oh alright! So many a times
I've let guests abuse their airtime
Freely broadcasting all their grime
Foolishly enthralled as I watched their crime

Great entertainers and as they perform
Their goal is to make me nod and conform
To make me think, feel and act on pure misinform
To destroy the true me beyond reform

Fun, captivating, it seemed a good deal
Suddenly all make-believe felt real
Frightening me constantly an ordeal
I failed to see intentions they conceal

Chaos, misery, depression and pain
That's all they bring nothing more to gain
So why give any precious space in my brain
I now choose who stays in my domain

Get out! Stay out! I rule! Don't you dare come near
The Sword of the Spirit is now part of my gear
It will show me your true face ever so clear
From hereon you're nothing but from my yesteryear

Proverbs 4:23
Common English Bible (CEB)

*More than anything you guard,
protect your mind, for life flows from it.*

Philippians 4:8
Amplified Bible (AMP)

*Finally, believers,
whatever is true, whatever is honorable and worthy of respect,
whatever is right and confirmed by God's word,
whatever is pure and wholesome,
whatever is lovely and brings peace,
whatever is admirable and of good repute;
if there is any excellence, if there is anything worthy of praise,
think continually on these things
[center your mind on them and implant them in your heart].*

Chapter 2: Deal with one box or less at a time

When I started my three-year journey with depression and anxiety, we had just transferred to another house. My mental state was a dark mess. My emotions were in disarray. Our living quarters were just as chaotic, as they were littered with boxes both opened and unopened. For weeks, I was paralyzed with fear and anxious thoughts. These were even compounded with the constant nagging guilt from not being able to clean up, deal with the boxes, or even cook a simple meal.

Occasionally I was forced to open a box to look for something the kids needed. Each time I had to do this, my hands would shake, my knees felt weak and I would have cold sweat breaking out on my face. I simply dreaded having to open a box and stare at all the stuff that needed putting away. I much preferred them unopened and just "avoid" the responsibility.

One day I really had to find something from one of the boxes. A few of them were not labeled, and that made the task so much more difficult. I couldn't help myself from sobbing as I began my search. I was alone in the house and so I felt free just crying my heart out as I rummaged through the boxes. First box, no luck. Second box couldn't find it.

Then I got to the third box. It was filled with our kitchen stuff: some pots and pans, cooking utensils, knives, spoons and forks, and some plates still wrapped in newspaper. I found what I was looking for and then-suddenly, I was conscious of a flutter in my heart. I unwrapped a few plates and laid them on the dining table and did the same with the spoons and forks. I took the pots and pans out and put them at their allotted spaces in the kitchen cabinets. After thirty minutes, I was halfway through the box having actually put the things away and not just left them scattered on the floor as I usually did.

I've always loved to cook, so seeing and touching my kitchenware again lifted my spirits in a way that I haven't felt in a long time. With my beloved pots and pans out, this still foreign kitchen suddenly doesn't seem so painfully unfamiliar anymore. But at that point, I was exhausted. I stared at the remaining kitchen items in the box and decided to call it a day.

That night in bed I recalled that feeling of elation and wondered whether I could again muster the strength to finish what remained in the box the next day. I prayed *"Lord God, for tomorrow, please give me the strength even for just half a box."*

What actually happened was this: No, I didn't finish the box the next day, but I did so several days after. I just took my time and after that half box came more boxes. I took all the time that I needed. There were days I could clear up only half a box. Certain boxes took several days to clear up. I took my cues from my available strength and didn't push myself beyond what I could do for the moment.

I always took time to take pleasure from having cleared a box. I never once allowed myself to feel bad for having to call it a day. Instead, I made sure to pat myself on the back for having accomplished my clearing task. I eventually cleared up all the boxes in a total of three months.

I cannot overstate the tremendous release I felt each time I cleared a box. It didn't just make the house cleaner; I was also mentally and emotionally a little less cluttered. Doing it almost equally amounted to clearing out my emotional and psychological cobwebs.

What I used to dread with so much anxiety has now been conquered.

Practical Guide:

1. Pray for strength. Then take your **flush-free** Niacin (Vitamin B3) and drink your buttered or heavily-creamed coffee or tea.

2. AND make yourself **willing** to do the work. In this chapter's meditation scripture, the people were three things: skilled, able and willing. They expressed their willingness by "coming". I expressed my willingness by: getting out of bed and walking to where the boxes were. Nothing happened **until** I did those two first, even when the strength or ability was there.

3. Don't be ashamed to skip days when you need to. I did. I just had to make sure that it was due to my being too weak and not being unwilling to work. As I did more and more work, I found out that I was able to distinguish between the two more easily.

4. Take notice of what lifts your spirit. During depression, everything is dark, but then any sliver of light is easily seen and felt. Whenever you feel or see that tiny sliver, grab it and see where it came from, and seek more of where it came from. I conquered my very first box because I sensed pleasure from seeing and touching my kitchen stuff again.

Yes, you **can do** it. One box or less at a time.

You're Just a Task

Nothing much about you really
Though you try hard to make it seem eerie
When I come near you to size you up
I see smallness that was just scaled up
Once I touch you, your enormity dissolves
Mere kittens pretending as wolves
Here I come, you I unmask
Now… see? You are simply a task

Exodus 36:2
New International Version (NIV)

*Then Moses summoned Bezalel and Oholiab
and every skilled person
to whom the Lord had given ability
and who was willing to come and do the work.*

Chapter 3: Let forgiveness start with your mouth

I started my 3-year journey through depression with so much anger and hatred in my heart. Although I knew that I was not without blame for the failure of our business venture, I found endless reasons to lay greater blame on our franchisors. I was having one of those days, when my sister visited me at home. We were having one of our let's-analyze-what-happened sessions, and I was just ranting about how our franchisors mercilessly pushed us into the gutter. I was feeling vindictive most especially for how they slandered us. I wanted to do the same thing to them. I wanted everyone to know what they did to us and how much they're responsible for the situation we were now in. I wanted to hurt their reputation just as much as they've hurt ours.

Then, all of a sudden, my sister laid her hand on my arm. It was so unexpected, and yet so gentle that the gesture made me stop from talking almost immediately. Right away I sensed what was coming even before my sister said the words. She said, *"I think, you and the bread baking business you're starting now will be blessed so much more if you will stop spreading anything negative about your franchisors."*

Through my sister, God had just asked me to start forgiving. It was the most difficult thing for me to do at that moment because everything in me wanted to do the opposite. But with His message, God provided the very first step towards forgiveness: stop talking about them. He wasn't asking me to forgive with my mind and heart right away. He knew it was a process. But I could start somewhere. I could start with my mouth.

I used to think that talking about these people and hating them was a privilege that I had for having been hurt and offended. But what surprised me was the immediate feeling of being relieved of a burden that I didn't even realize I was carrying. Talking and ranting about people who offended me was a heavy burden that I carried, and I didn't even know that until I was free. Until I let go.

Practical Guide:

1. Read the meditation verse slowly, over and over. Notice how more relaxed you feel each time you read. I always do each time I read those.

2. One deterrent that had always helped me avoid any verbal spite is this mental activity: everything that you want to say about the people who have offended you, think about them, form the words, BUT only in your head. Let those words and sentences play in a constant loop in your mind. Imagine saying those words in person, to that person, over and over. Each time I did this exercise, I felt spent and satisfied, but more importantly, thankful that it was all just an imagination, that my words have not really done any further and permanent damage. Then I thank God for imaginations.

It's a long road. But you can definitely let forgiveness **start** with your mouth.

Double-Edged

A double-edged sword this thing called offense
Varied forms it takes but words are most intense
Spoken with much gusto and passionate cadence
To a carefully-selected, ever-willing audience
It harms the speaker as much as the subject, hence
It is called a double-edged tongue of offense

Matthew 11:29-30
21st Century King James Version

Take My yoke upon you and learn of Me,
for I am meek and lowly in heart,
and ye shall find rest unto your souls.
For My yoke is easy, and My burden is light

Matthew 11:29-30
Easy-to-Read Version

Accept my teaching. Learn from me.
I am gentle and humble in spirit.
And you will be able to get some rest.
Yes, the teaching that I ask you to accept is easy.
The load I give you to carry is light.

Chapter 4: Face yourself

Face yourself. There's one person in the world that we often find hard to face. The Man in the mirror. Ourselves. It can be because we're so busy facing and looking at other people or we simply refuse to look at ourselves. Maybe it's because we're afraid to acknowledge the many flaws that we have. In my case, being maliciously offended and slandered made it extra difficult for me to see my own true colors. I thought *"none of my mistakes could come close to the magnitude of what they've done to me"*.

However, since the day I made that commitment to stop talking about the people who have offended me, my inner world was suddenly much quieter. I found more wiggle room for me to turn and face myself. It took many months before I could finally and comfortably see and look at myself for what I was, and all the mistakes that I did. It was painful and looking at mine was like rubbing sand paper against my own wound.

Surely, looking at others' faults was far easier. But then here's what I realized: it doesn't help me or my situation. It has dawned on me that I do have a shot at making a difference with my situation if I try to look at my own mistakes. After all, I have better chances at changing the person I am with 24/7. Me.

A great author, H. Jackson Brown Jr., once wrote *"Let the refining and improving of your own life keep you so busy that you have little time to criticize others."*

I was so desperate for my situation to change, that changing myself immediately became a welcome idea, no matter how painful a process I knew it would be.

Practical Guide:

The Message's translation of the meditations scripture really cut deep into my heart. Again, it's painful, but I have come to appreciate pain. And you can too. I have also learned to equate pain with rewards, then later, with relief. That is what I encourage you to take from this: to expect relief after pain. It's so much like when we're trying to clean our eyes from dust or dirt. There's a burning pain while the dirt is there. But as soon as we've cleared it out, there is much relief.

To see clearly the beam in your own eye, you **must face yourself.**

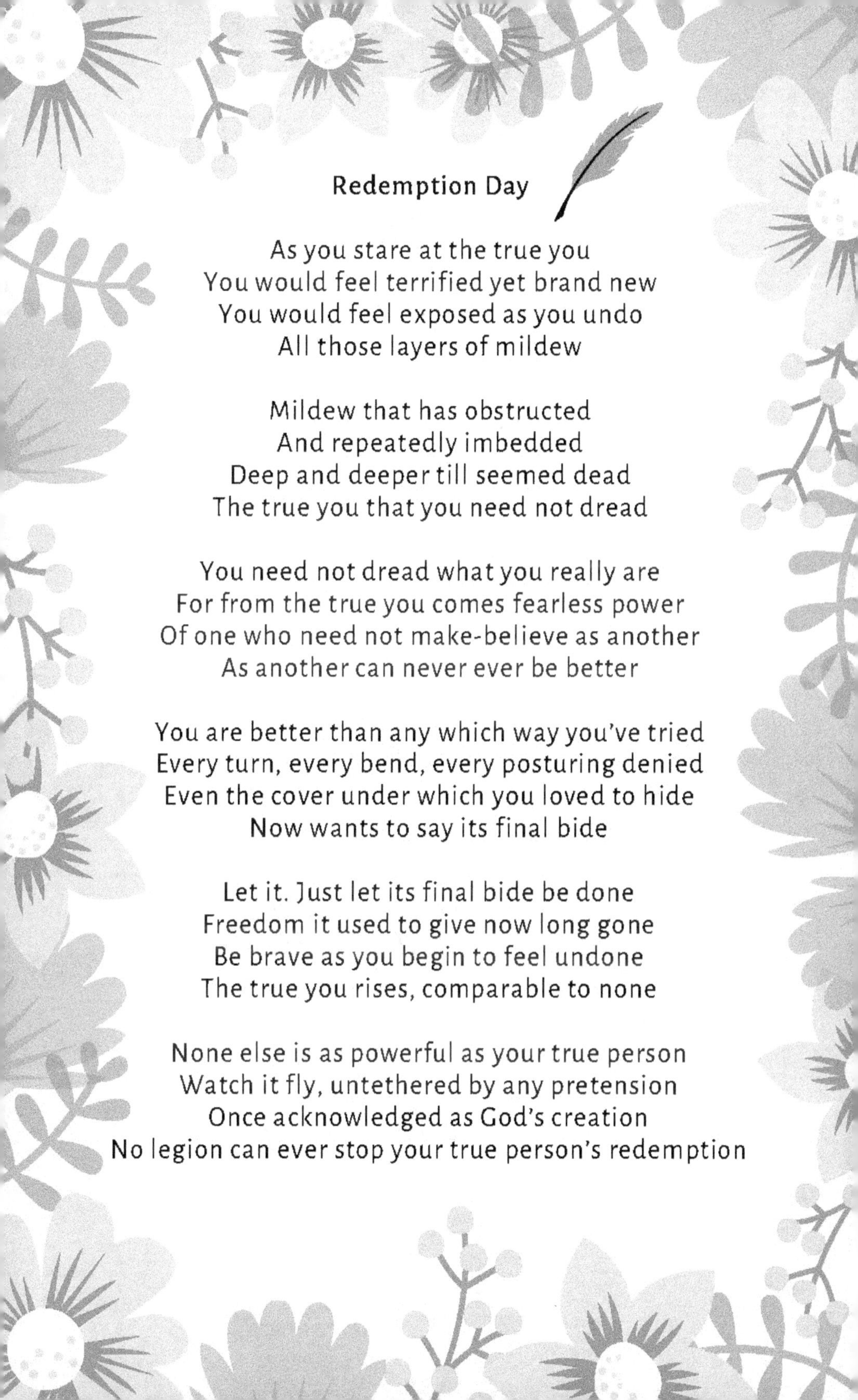

Redemption Day

As you stare at the true you
You would feel terrified yet brand new
You would feel exposed as you undo
All those layers of mildew

Mildew that has obstructed
And repeatedly imbedded
Deep and deeper till seemed dead
The true you that you need not dread

You need not dread what you really are
For from the true you comes fearless power
Of one who need not make-believe as another
As another can never ever be better

You are better than any which way you've tried
Every turn, every bend, every posturing denied
Even the cover under which you loved to hide
Now wants to say its final bide

Let it. Just let its final bide be done
Freedom it used to give now long gone
Be brave as you begin to feel undone
The true you rises, comparable to none

None else is as powerful as your true person
Watch it fly, untethered by any pretension
Once acknowledged as God's creation
No legion can ever stop your true person's redemption

Matthew 7:5
Amplified Bible (AMP)

You hypocrite (play-actor, pretender),
first get the log out of your own eye,
and then you will see clearly
to take the speck out of your brother's eye.

Matthew 7:5
The Message (MSG)

A Simple Guide for Behavior
Don't pick on people, jump on their failures, criticize their faults—
unless, of course, you want the same treatment.
That critical spirit has a way of boomeranging.
It's easy to see a smudge on your neighbor's face
and be oblivious to the ugly sneer on your own.
Do you have the nerve to say, 'Let me wash your face for you,'
when your own face is distorted by contempt?
It's this whole traveling road-show mentality all over again,
playing a holier-than-thou part instead of just living your part.
Wipe that ugly sneer off your own face,
and you might be fit to offer a washcloth to your neighbor.

Chapter 5: Sulk if you must

I cannot count how often I blamed and nagged myself with words like: "If only I had listened…", "I should not have done this, and that…", "Had I taken time to do this, I would not have…".

I'd reach the end of the day having spent hours with self-blame, tired and exhausted and yet find myself doing the same thing again the next day. At this stage of my depressed years, I had received dozens of counselling on: not to feel condemned by our past; forgetting what lies behind and striving for what lies ahead; using our mistakes as tools to make ourselves better; etc. And still, there I was, with my "what ifs" and "I should not haves", almost on a daily basis.

The thing was, I kept indulging in these "regret sessions" of mine, because, at that point, I didn't feel condemned for making those mistakes anymore. And secondly, I refused to forget my mistakes because there was something in me that told me that doing that would be more tragic.

And lastly, it felt liberating. Have you ever tried to get rid of a pus-filled acne? Or clean out an infected leg wound? I don't know with you, but I don't stop until everything is out. Everything. I wasn't satisfied until I see clear fluid coming out as I squeezed. And each time I stopped halfway because of the pain, it was much more inflamed and swollen the next day.

Sulking in your regrets doesn't mean you let yourself drown in them. For me, it afforded me to know those places so well that I could spot them miles ahead and avoid them. More importantly, I've oriented myself thoroughly with my mistakes, that now, I can lead people around to avoid them, and towards the better and regret-free way.

Practical Guide:

There is a trap you must be careful not to fall into while you're in one of your regret sessions. I call it the "zombie trap". It's when you try to do your daily chores while your mind is in a regret session, and you move and work while just being half aware of the people around you, not just physically but also emotionally. Hence, you end up not being sensitive to them, and possibly hurting them. It's the trap I fell into when I snapped at my son while I was washing the dishes and he was asking me a question, repeatedly, because I wasn't hearing him, having let myself deeply into a regret session. That is why it is very important to have these regret sessions completely in private: with nothing else and no one else except yourself. Do it when the kids are in school or out, husband is at work and chores are out of the way.

Position yourself in a corner, as comfortably as you can. Then… **sulk if you must**.

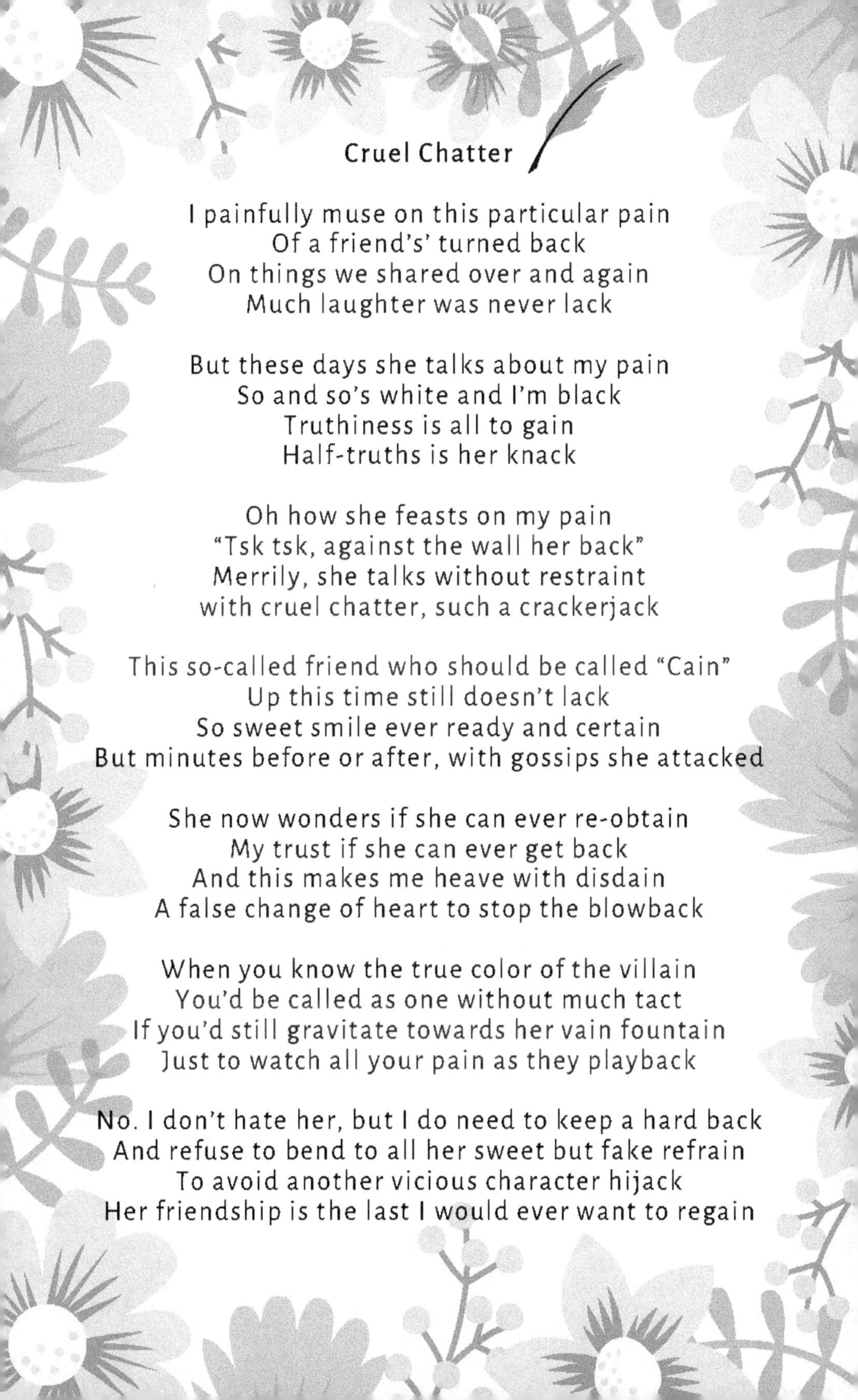

Cruel Chatter

I painfully muse on this particular pain
Of a friend's' turned back
On things we shared over and again
Much laughter was never lack

But these days she talks about my pain
So and so's white and I'm black
Truthiness is all to gain
Half-truths is her knack

Oh how she feasts on my pain
"Tsk tsk, against the wall her back"
Merrily, she talks without restraint
with cruel chatter, such a crackerjack

This so-called friend who should be called "Cain"
Up this time still doesn't lack
So sweet smile ever ready and certain
But minutes before or after, with gossips she attacked

She now wonders if she can ever re-obtain
My trust if she can ever get back
And this makes me heave with disdain
A false change of heart to stop the blowback

When you know the true color of the villain
You'd be called as one without much tact
If you'd still gravitate towards her vain fountain
Just to watch all your pain as they playback

No. I don't hate her, but I do need to keep a hard back
And refuse to bend to all her sweet but fake refrain
To avoid another vicious character hijack
Her friendship is the last I would ever want to regain

Lamentations 3:40
Common English Bible (CEB)

We must search and examine our ways;
we must return to the Lord.

Psalm 119:59
New Living Translation (NLT)

I pondered the direction of my life,
and I turned to follow your laws.

Psalm 139:23-24
New American Standard Bible (NASB)

Search me, O God, and know my heart;
Try me and know my anxious thoughts;
And see if there be any hurtful way in me,
And lead me in the everlasting way.

Chapter 6: Give what is due

A couple of years before we suffered bankruptcy, a friend visited me at home and noticed our stack of pirated movie DVDs. She stared at them for a while, as if contemplating something in her mind. Finally, she said, *"You know what Rose, since we stopped buying pirated DVDs, God has worked miracles in our lives especially in our finances. Really, buying pirated DVDs is actually no different from stealing. And stealing, in the eyes of God, is a sin. And sins have consequences."*

I didn't pay much attention to what my friend said. I continued to buy pirated DVDs, thinking *"Well we can't afford to pay for cinema tickets or to purchase original DVDs, so this must be ok"*. Then 2008 came and my depression and anxiety attacks began. One day, while meditating on Luke 6:31, I found myself thinking about my friend's uneventful visit, and what she said just kept playing in my head in a constant loop for hours. Before the day ended, I made up my mind and made a promise to God that I would never, ever again, give in to the temptation of buying pirated DVDs.

It was a decision that was much harder to keep during those days when my two bored sons were bugging me to go out and buy some pirated DVDs. They were young then and couldn't grasp the concept of righteousness and doing good to your neighbors. But I held my ground and kept explaining to them that it is wrong. I kept saying that if we stayed faithful, that God would eventually enable us financially to afford going to the cinema or buy original DVDs.

We also stopped borrowing pirated DVDs from friends and neighbors. I also prohibited my sons from buying and borrowing pirated games for their play station and watching pirated movies online. It was a tough period for us, and I constantly prayed for God to help us stay contented with whatever is available on cable TV.

Five years later, in 2013, not only were we financially able to treat ourselves for occasional cinema and purchase original DVDs, but we also witnessed how God expanded our bread baking classes business from the original hands-on set-up to online videos. That's right. Online videos that people **pay** us to watch. Isn't the coincidence obvious? Being able to offer online videos anywhere in the world to anyone who wanted to learn bakery bread baking was beyond our wildest dreams for our business. We were happy to earn from giving hands-on classes to 3 to 6 students at a time. But God is a God who rewards His faithful. And time and again, I would remind my kids and husband that the blessings we're experiencing now is a direct result of all our sacrifices. We have paid our dues but we must stay faithful.

Practical Guide:

1. If you're going through the same struggle, take time to read these articles:
    a. Is Digital Piracy Really a Sin?
       https://lifehopeandtruth.com/change/blog/is-digital-piracy-really-a-sin/
    b. What does the Bible say about digital piracy?
       https://www.ucg.org/bible-study-aids/bible-questions-and-answers/what-does-the-bible-say-about-digital-piracy
2. With your children, it's best to start early. Show them the links above and if possible, read the articles together.
3. If you have victories in life, big or small, draw your family's attention to them, pointing out that it could have been because of your faithfulness in honoring your neighbor.
4. Assess your life and see if there is any other area where you need to practice the same principle of "giving what is due". The following questions might help:
    a. If you're an employer, do you owe an employee his due wage? Do you give it on time? Do you ask for far and above

the agreed "scope of work", always thinking that you should have your "money's worth"?

b. Or are you an employee who clocks in "on time" but steals paid time for things not related to your work, like doing online social networking such as Facebook, etc., during work hours. Or maybe wasting away work hours on phone calls not related to work. Or do you engage in "pilferage"? Pilferage means stealing in "small amounts", which can make one think that he's not doing any harm. For example, does it still bother your conscience when you bring home a pad of paper, or a box of paper clips, or use your company's Xerox machine for your own personal use? Do you correctly and honestly declare reimbursable expenses? **When you get something that doesn't belong to you, whether time, goods or money, you are "stealing".**

c. Have you made a promise to someone and have not fulfilled it even if you have been and still are able to fulfill it? The moment you made that promise, you created for yourself a "due" and unless you ask the person you made the promise to, to "free" you from the promise, then you have to fulfill it. This, of course, includes unpaid debts.

5. Finally, encourage your family to study these verses:

Psalm 19:7-8,11 New American Standard Bible (NASB)

This is one reason why I love reading the Word of God. I love its practicality for life, for day-to-day application. It shows me things as they are: what happens if I do things I shouldn't do, if I don't do things I ought to do, the general rules for life that is free from heartaches and pains. I realized it is such foolishness to think that I could continue "shortchanging" my neighbor, a friend, my government, or a billionaire who owns a record or movie company and continue living my life without anticipating my actions' boomeranging back to me.

I would rather give what is due now than be asked an interest over a principal later on.

Give what is due to others and God will give what is due **to you.**

Beyond This

Oh, how taken we are with the current view
Not even noticing it has gone askew
We've gotten so used to it like beloved leather shoes
Not realizing our toes have merely become callous

There is another side, beyond our present horizon
Another still that lies in the opposite direction
Both remain unseen, waiting for us to change our gaze
Until then, we cannot enjoy the new bountiful graze

Luke 6:31
New American Standard Bible (NASB)

Treat others the same way
you want them to treat you.

Chapter 7: Let mercy and grace heal

A few nights ago, I told my son "The repairman came and changed your bedroom doorknob. By the way, may I borrow your lampshade for a while? While repairing my headboard, the repairman tripped on my lampshade and broke the glass-shade to pieces."

There was a pause and then my son asked, *"Well did you charge him for it, Mommy?"* And I said *"No, of course not. He came to work and earn money. He didn't mean to break my lampshade."*

Another quiet pause followed, and I said *"Babe, I showed him mercy and grace. Mercy and grace. That's what he needed and that's what I gave."*

And my son said *"Yes mommy I understand. I love you."*

That's me, today.

But I was far from that way, ten years ago. Around that time, prior to the start of my depression years, I was an eye-for-an-eye-here's-what-you-deserve kind of person. I wasn't mean, but certainly I wasn't gracious either. When a cashier at a department store failed to smile or be polite, I made it a point to "courteously" tell her that it was her duty to smile at all customers no matter how she felt. Today, whenever I notice a sad employee, I immediately try to feel their pain, and in that very short period of opportunity, do my best to bring a smile to their face. Almost always, though, a simple, but sincere smile is enough to make them smile back.

Had the incident with my lampshade happened back then, I would certainly have charged it against the repairman's salary, after a good, long lecture on being careful.

By the way, when I saw the broken pieces of my lampshade on the floor, I heard the repairman mutter under his breath, *"it's not even enough…"* referring to his day's wage not being enough to cover the damage. Immediately, I told him *"Accidents happen. Don't worry about it Manong Junior."* Then, I paid him his full wage and gave him two bags of used t-shirts, which he accepted with teary eyes.

What I did was give Manong Junior enough reasons to be just as merciful and just as gracious to somebody else. During those three years of anxiety and depression, God taught me a lot about mercy and grace. And that lesson served as one of my major healing pills. I learned about them quickly because I received them first in large doses. I was a greedy recipient of God's mercy and grace. I needed them badly because I knew how disgustingly it felt to have been a disappointment.

Indeed, it felt amazing to receive God's mercy and grace. But that was just the first half of the pill. The other half is "giving" back mercy and grace. That made this healing pill whole and powerful. Each time I show somebody mercy and grace, a certain amount of darkness is lifted off. It has provided an undeniable feeling of relief that has actually made the exercise easier and easier to do, as more opportunities come to me to be merciful and gracious to someone.

Practical Guide:

I've found out that the best way to stay merciful is to follow it up immediately with grace. That really seals the deal. When I was preparing Manong Junior's salary, I thought of giving him some old t-shirts that he could still make good use of in his construction work. Giving him his salary in full was being merciful. Giving him an extra gift was being gracious, and that for sure made Manong Junior realize that I truly had forgiven him for breaking my lampshade.

Let what has healed you, **heal others** as well: mercy and grace.

Grace Completes Mercy

Without grace,
mercy is like a balloon propped up by a stiff stick
Not free and bouncy when it's just a candlewick

Without grace,
mercy is like a handshake offered generously
but devoid of smile to say it was given happily

Without grace,
mercy is like a tree with much leaves, but no fruits
"Come, under me take shade. But nothing more than that.", it hoots

And without grace,
mercy can only say "I forgive you. Goodbye."
and never "I forgive you. We can give it another try."

Psalm 103:10-12
New American Standard Bible (NASB)

He has not dealt with us according to our sins,
Nor rewarded us according to our iniquities.
For as high as the heavens are above the earth,
So great is His loving kindness toward those who fear Him.
As far as the east is from the west,
So far has He removed our transgressions from us.

Chapter 8: Get Diagnosed, then Heal from "Immediate-itis"

As I write this chapter, our church, Christ Commission Fellowship, is presently teaching the congregation a series on spiritual "landmines". One of the topics from the series is titled "Beware of Immediate-ITIS, wait on the Lord", and this is the short description on the Sunday worship video: *"We live in this fast-paced world, where everything is instant. We are in a fast food, and microwave society where we want everything now. Honestly, life is full of waiting, though we are programmed to believe that we should never have to wait for anything. It is so difficult to wait when we have the knowledge, experience and ability to take action on our own."*

Many of my problems were results of my inability to wait. In my desire to have our own business, I let myself be carried away by the promise of having a bakery that sells thousands of breads daily. I thought *"if this worked for our friends, then it should work for us"*. I failed to analyze that there is a big gap between dream and reality, and it is called "planning". I failed to do my due diligence. Wikipedia defines due diligence as *"an investigation of a business or person prior to signing a contract, or an act with a certain standard of care"*. I failed because I didn't do enough investigation, and I didn't exercise enough care. I stepped right smack on the landmine of immediate-itis and when it blew up, it disintegrated everything; our reputation, all our savings, and it created a crater of debt that took us years to pay.

Today, I can freely say all these, without pain or difficulty, 10 years after it happened. But back then, just months after I stepped on the landmine, I was a nervous wreck, and too afraid to touch anything, having lost my confidence almost completely. My immediate-itis progressed further to paralysis.

The day came that I finally decided to revisit the site of destruction. I looked look at it in the face and analyzed the path that I had taken to get there. Looking at that big crater and acknowledging that my being impatient and succumbing to "immediate-itis", had a lot to do with the destruction, was the very first step towards my healing from immediate-itis. It's not at all that different from healing from an actual physical disease. You acknowledge that you have it and try to analyze how you got there. Then you try to stop the progress of the disease by avoiding the same path you took that got you the disease in the first place.

Remember that scripture about taking the beam out of your own eye before looking at the speck in another person's eye? Acknowledging my immediate-itis, was like chopping off a big portion off that beam in my eye.

Practical Guide:

1. When you go through any process of self-analysis, you will constantly stumble on roadblocks called "condemnation". You know that you've tripped over it when all you could ask and tell yourself is "How could you have done this?" or "This is all your fault. You should have known better", and so on. Whenever this happened to me, I let my imagination work. Yes, I tripped, but I still got my two legs and arms, so I push my palms against the floor and get back up on my feet and continue my journey while reciting the verse from 1 John 1:9 "If we confess our sins, He is faithful and righteous to forgive us our sins and to cleanse us from all unrighteousness."
2. Remember to take daily dosage of No-flush Niacin and Vitamin C.

Heal from "Immediate-ITIS". Do it **now**.

Bomb of Life

Here's a bomb, and it might explode
You're asking me to hand it to you
Know that I know all about its code
Just like mine had, this one has too

Relax. You cannot be miscalculating
Remember, it's a bomb, it might go "ka-boom!"
The one I had I thought would go "ka-ching!"
Instead it blasted me into a 3-year gloom

Now, come closer and look. Do you see?
Do you see all the twisting and turning?
Do you see how deceptive and tricky?
That's what you'll be getting into hopefully without burning

Do you really want it- this explosive?
Do you have what it takes to handle it with care?
To dismantle it you have to skillfully achieve
Or you might as well not dare

It's a risk you don't have to take
So why do you want it in the first place?
Possessing it a person doesn't make
Knowing how to have it can still bring menace

So, what now is your decision?
I can teach you the code and all
Your lust for it, is it still on?
50/50 chance, are you still willing to gamble?

Proverbs 21:5
Amplified Bible (AMP)

*The plans of the diligent lead surely to
abundance and advantage,
But everyone who acts in haste
comes surely to poverty.*

Proverbs 19:2
The Message (MSG)

*Ignorant zeal is worthless;
Haste makes waste.*

Chapter 9: Realize that you can move with fear

One day I woke up. It was again 2 a.m. Though the room was cold with the air-conditioning on, my face was drenched with sweat. I just had another bad dream, which, most often, I couldn't remember. My throat was so dry, and I needed a glass of water, but I couldn't get up from bed. I had to wait to feel my knees and legs. I could feel my heart and it was pounding like crazy in my chest and ears. I was looking down at my shirt and I could see the fabric vibrating against my skin with each loud beat of my heart. I was panting and every so second, I could feel my chest sucking as much air as I could.

I felt dreadful and alone, as I always did each time I woke up from sleep, so immediately I focused my mind on reality. Where was I? I was in my bedroom. Who was I with in the house? My two sons. Where were they? They were in their room sleeping. Thinking about them brought the strength back to my knees and I pulled myself from bed and walked towards my sons' bedroom. I opened their door and saw them. They were there sleeping soundly. I looked at them for a long time and started thanking God for them.

I still felt weak. My heart was still beating loudly. I got myself a cold glass of water and drank it slowly, noting how pleasant the feel of the cold water running down my throat. I rubbed my chest. As always, it felt like there was a knife stuck in my heart.

As each minute passed, more and more realities of my life started rushing back into my mind. Other bitter anxieties started sucking this strength away from my knees: one of our debtors called the other day and I was almost sure she would call again today; my sons' tuition fees were due very soon which meant I had to remind my husband again about it; we were four months behind our car's amortization, and I had to decide soon when to call the bank about our decision to return the car, instead of it being pulled from the garage.

I felt weak again, so I grabbed the dining chair and sat down. Right in front me, in a big pile on the dining table were our fresh clothes that needed folding. Though my arms felt both heavy and weak, I lifted them up, picked up a piece of clothing, stretched it on the table and started folding. I picked another t-shirt, stretched it on the table, folded the sides and laid it on top of the first one. I did the same thing with the 3rd piece, and so on and so forth. After 2 hours, I had finished folding all the clothes. I noticed how neat and straight the sides were.

I realized that I had just **done something productive**, despite my pain, my dread, and all the fears that hounded my heart. I started something, and I finished it. I sat there and stared at those neatly folded clothes. Though I couldn't stretch my lips to smile, I noticed I had stopped crying. I actually felt better than I did two hours earlier.

This is one of the many important realizations I held on to during the first few months of my depression. I realized that even though many times I felt like just staying in bed, too weak to move, even too weak to speak or eat; I didn't have to do just how I felt. I can do more than that. I can actually feel how I felt and still do things no matter how small they were.

It can be just washing some dirty plates, or wiping a surface clean, or throwing the trash, or making your bed.

One time, it started raining and I hurriedly grabbed our drying clothes from the line and threw them on the bed. I collapsed on the bed breathless. I told myself "That's ok. I managed to save the clothes from getting soaked by the rain!" I did something and more importantly, I felt good about it!

Though doing a chore always left me temporarily exhausted, it lighted a fuse inside me. I realized that I can still be productive. I know now that I didn't have to be totally useless. Don't listen to your fear. It's enough that you feel it. You don't need to be "it". You just have to pray for strength and believe that you have it.

Practical Guide:

1. Each time you finish a chore, no matter how simple it is, tap yourself on the back and say, "You did great."

2. Take note of things that give you even the tiniest relief and do those more often. Drinking a very cold glass of water has always relieved my tight and dry throat and it has also helped bring down my body's temperature.

3. Continue to take flush-free Niacin (Vitamin B3). I take 2 capsules of 500mg every night. In my first book: Depression and Intense Anxieties: Your Quickest Way Out, I wrote about how Niacin had helped me and my family deal not just with depression but also with our bad tempers.

4. Each and every time I woke from sleep feeling much dread, there was nothing else, no basis to connect to the dread and intense fear. For several minutes I couldn't even remember our problems. All I felt was that very physical pain in my chest and those very strong ominous sensations in my gut. But I couldn't answer the question "why do I feel this way?" at least until I have progressed during the day. The point that you feel the most dread is the point you need to force yourself to:

    1) focus and zero in on positive realities,
    2) and then count your blessings.

    No matter how cliché that sounded, you must do it. Fear *only* makes you feel hopeless. My children are enough reason for me to "re-feel" hope. The moment I started re-feeling hope is the moment I began feeling **less** fear.

Yes, you can **move even with fear**.

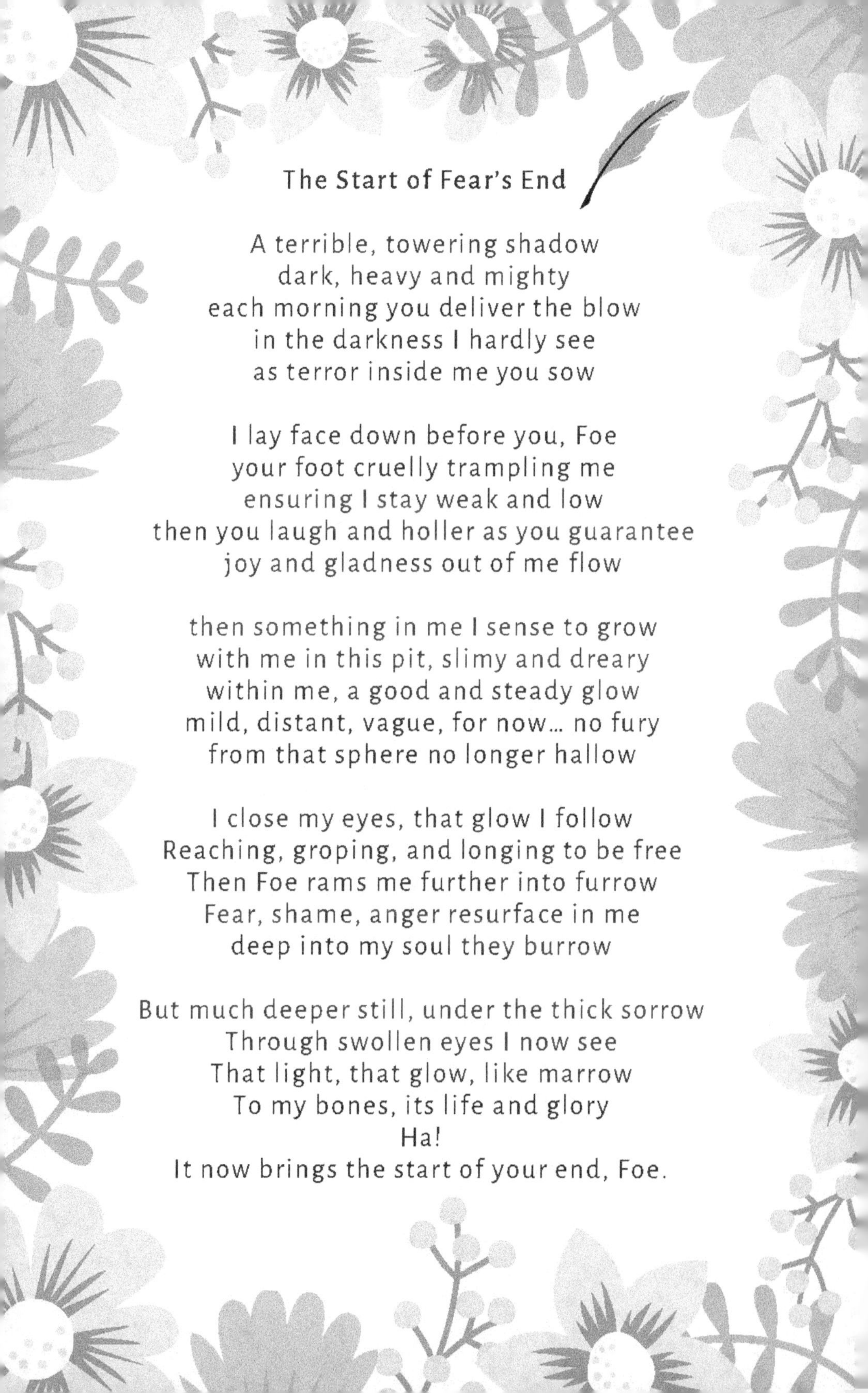

The Start of Fear's End

A terrible, towering shadow
dark, heavy and mighty
each morning you deliver the blow
in the darkness I hardly see
as terror inside me you sow

I lay face down before you, Foe
your foot cruelly trampling me
ensuring I stay weak and low
then you laugh and holler as you guarantee
joy and gladness out of me flow

then something in me I sense to grow
with me in this pit, slimy and dreary
within me, a good and steady glow
mild, distant, vague, for now… no fury
from that sphere no longer hallow

I close my eyes, that glow I follow
Reaching, groping, and longing to be free
Then Foe rams me further into furrow
Fear, shame, anger resurface in me
deep into my soul they burrow

But much deeper still, under the thick sorrow
Through swollen eyes I now see
That light, that glow, like marrow
To my bones, its life and glory
Ha!
It now brings the start of your end, Foe.

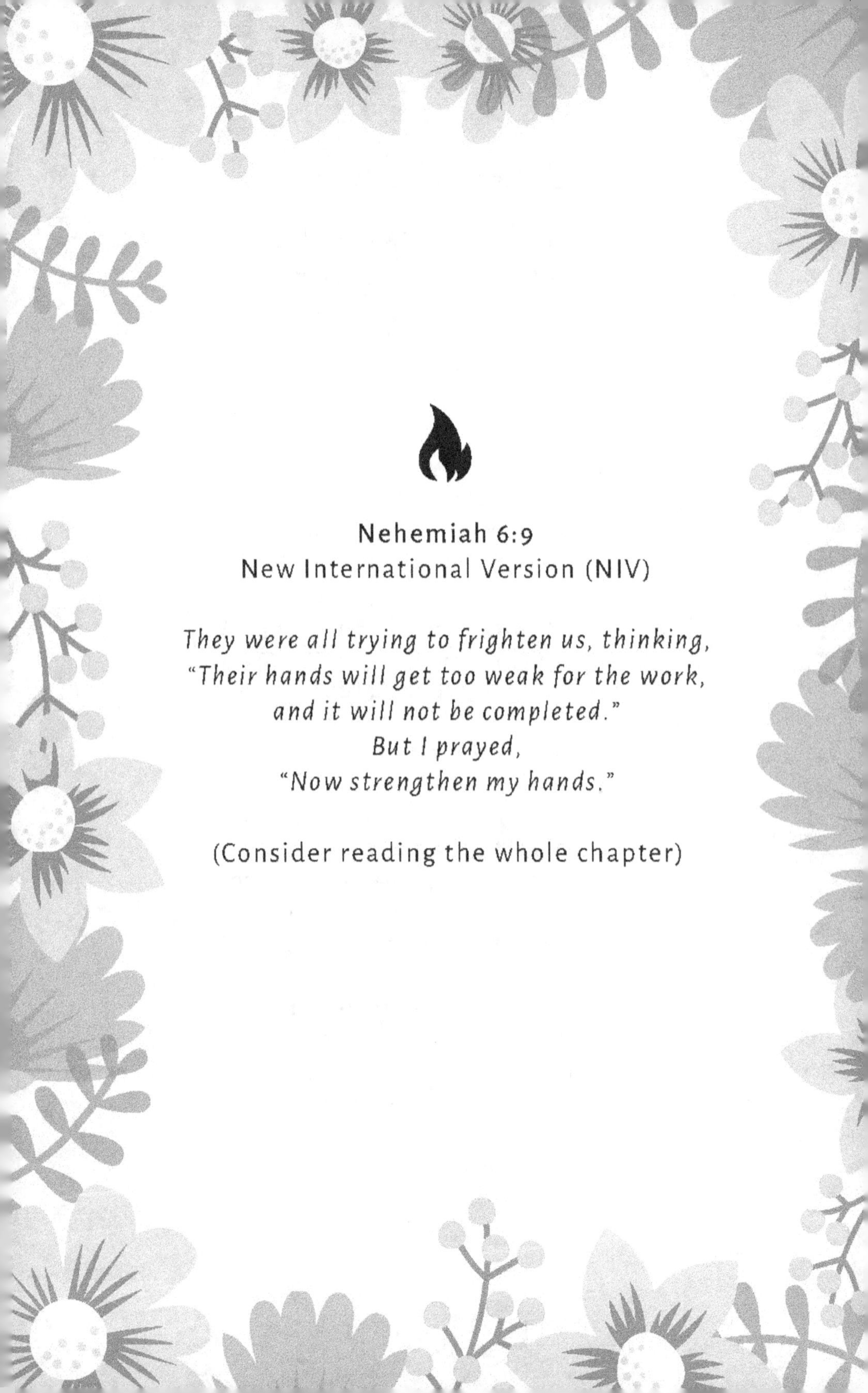

Nehemiah 6:9
New International Version (NIV)

*They were all trying to frighten us, thinking,
"Their hands will get too weak for the work,
and it will not be completed."
But I prayed,
"Now strengthen my hands."*

(Consider reading the whole chapter)

Chapter 10: Whatever works, work it

Several months into my depression, I found out that taking long baths and submerging in the bathtub gave me both physical and emotional relief. My heartbeats were slower, the "knife" feeling in my chest wasn't as painful, and my mind wasn't racing with negative thoughts. I would stretch my bath time as long as I could. I usually had them when the kids were in school, and especially when I knew I'd be all alone. Often, during the summer, I would drain and replace the water up to three times in my efforts to keep my body cool. This activity was one of the very few I had to look forward to each day.

Depression made me acutely aware of pain. I was constantly in agony; physically, mentally, and emotionally. When everything was black, dark and heavy, any snippet of white or light was magnified and easily felt and seen. I grabbed onto anything that provided my body relief from pain. Taking long baths, being submerged in cool water was one, and drinking cold water was another. Somebody I know, who also suffered from depression, would wet his feet whenever he felt so fearful and he did so several times a day.

Another thing that gave me comfort were pillows; soft ones. On my bed, I had two body pillows which were both five feet long, and two head pillows. I also had two blankets; a thick one when I felt colder and a thinner blanket for not-so-cold nights. I wanted to be as comfortable as I could be because either way, that would help me fall asleep or to get through the night fully awake. I tossed and turned during the night and anything that would help me feel comfortable was a big relief.

For this chapter's scripture meditation, we see Moses' arms getting tired from holding up his hands very long as the battle were fought. His hands needed to stay up, so they did something to help Moses. They did something very practical and it worked.

Practical Guide:

1. At the time I wrote this entry, there was news about a teenage girl who died after being accidentally electrocuted in the bathtub. She was found holding her cellphone which was still plugged in the electrical outlet on the wall. So please take caution. Better that you put away your cellphone while you're in the tub. Just take this time to relax and to feel your heart's rate go down and your hands and legs just being weightless in the water.

2. If you don't have a bathtub to soak in, then take showers as often as you want. You may also bring a comfortable chair in your bathroom and then submerge your legs in a pail of water. I have done that as well. I even put some ice in the water and that was really comforting.

Whatever works, work it.

A Moment of Rest

Lying in your arms I find rest
A pause, a break, the briefest of ease
Let me have this time so blest
For always and never cease

But life's calls and behest
From this rest now end of lease
As I rise out of you with heavy chest
I savor and long for my next release

Exodus 17:12
New International Version (NIV)

*When Moses' hands grew tired,
they took a stone and put it under him, and he sat
on it.
Aaron and Hur held his hands up
one on one side, one on the other
so that his hands remained steady till sunset.*

Chapter 11: Just Do. It doesn't have to be much.

One morning, I made my bed while in it. There I was lying in bed and feeling very weak. I had very little sleep. My heart was pounding in my ears the whole night and it jolted me awake every ten minutes. Again, I was awake at two in the morning, but I just kept my eyes shut. I tossed and turned and tried everything to doze back to sleep, but nothing worked. It was dawn when I finally opened my eyes. I was at the edge of the bed, and my blanket and two pillows were on the floor. Once more, I closed my eyes, and forced myself to breathe deeply but less frequently.

When I felt calmer, I opened my eyes and started reaching for the pillows and dragged each one from the floor onto the bed. Those simple movements sent my heart racing again and so I paused and took deep breaths for several minutes. Next, I pulled the blanket from the floor. Then I pulled my legs from the bed down to the floor and tried to sit on the edge of the bed, but I felt dizzy and my vision turned black. I fell back on the bed and waited several minutes for the wave of nausea to subside.

I realized I will have to make my bed while in it, and I refused not doing so for that day. If I have to stay in bed making it, then so be it. It took me thirty painful minutes to make my bed, but I finally did it. The blanket wasn't folded as nicely as I wanted to, but it was neat enough for that moment. The pillows were on top of each other and the sheet was stretched as flat as I could manage. I was satisfied. **I conquered my bed!**

Practical Guide:

1. Desire to do something that you can do and then finish it. I found it extremely helpful to "rehearse" mentally the steps or actions I needed to make in starting and completing any chore. A lot of times I did these mental rehearsals repeatedly until the steps "felt" easy enough to do. These mental rehearsals certainly unmasked the fear of doing the thing and at many instances I was surprised to realize how small and easy the task actually was compared to how, initially, I "felt" it was.

2. Never regard anything as ordinary or of no importance. Remember, in climbing a long ladder, one always has to start with the very first step.

3. Gauge first your level of energy before considering doing anything. Work with whatever amount of energy you have. During this stage, completing a task is so much more important than starting it. In my case, it rekindled in me a sense of purpose. When I start something, anyone else can finish it. But when I start something AND finish it, then no one else can do the "finishing" for me. I achieved the purpose in "finishing" the task, not starting it. Hence, it made sense to choose tasks that I could start AND finish. I pushed down my bars of standard, so I could reach them. Reaching a bar, however low it was, gave me more relief and satisfaction than doing something bigger halfway and unfinished.

Just **do**. It *really* doesn't have to be much.

Vortex of Despair

Sucked in a torturous vortex, at times under
At times wedged in undersides of blackness
Never out, never over
Sinking in despair, and aimlessness

Knew but can't remember better
In this seemingly permanent mess
Shameful, pitiless no abettor
So low I cannot be any less

Who I was seem not to matter
Who I am now devoid of brightness
Slandered, avoided like a leper
By friends now compassionless

Tossed here, there, up and under
No let up, constant restlessness
Searched but no relief anywhere
Predators feasting on my messes

Oh let them be, let me be, don't alter
Let time see who is true and deservingness
Stay in this vortex until I can no longer
Once out, I'll be clean, one of wholeness

2 Corinthians 8:11
New International Version (NIV)

*Now finish the work,
so that your eager willingness to do it
may be matched by your completion of it,
according to your means.*

Chapter 12: Mind what you watch

How you pass the time during the day can make or break your night or sleeping time. I learned the hard way that a lot of what aggravated my anxieties at night came from what I had heard and seen during the day. The media, particularly the television gave me these feelings of restlessness, uneasiness, and apprehensions. It didn't take long for me to figure out which TV programs could easily make me feel so much more anxious, so I made it a point to avoid them and preferred to watch instead Christian shows or positive programs that lifted my spirits. I also avoided commercials that veered on any type of violence or even just loud speech.

Whenever the TV was turned on whether I was alone or not, the remote control was always in my hand…always!

Having realized that how much of what I hear and see reverberates in my head especially when I'm in solitude, I've decided to "barricade" my mind and ears and to be **consciously aware** of the things that I **allow** to come in.

No one can do this for you except you. You must take responsibility for what lodges into your being. When I did, I had more control of what triggers my anxious thoughts.

Practical Guide:

Determine the television programs that give you pleasure and make you feel happier and take note of their time slots. This suggestion may seem so trivial, but I'm going to say it anyway: work your daily chores around these TV programs. At the onset of my depression, all my routine activities vanished. I had no energy nor the desire to do anything, so when I started to re-explore the television (cable or Netflix, or whatever you've got), I soon found myself thinking *"Oh I don't want to miss that program again. I better set my alarm."*

You see, after weeks and weeks of wanting to do nothing, reminding myself to "set my alarm" was a big improvement for me. This period, no matter how insignificant it now seems, was my re-introduction to some form of structure. It served some sort of a brake that helped break my swift and slippery slide down the slope of depression. Looking forward to something that I knew would give me some respite felt like a helpful crutch through my chores during the waiting time.

But then again, avoid anything that makes your heart troubled and make sure that you mind what you watch. (take this same caution for what you read and listen to).

Be careful. **Mind** what you watch.

Standing Guard

When suffering and tears come to mind
This stronghold of thoughts I now bind
Its doors and windows I hunt and find
Their eyes I render blind

Philippians 4:8-9
New International Version (NIV)

*Finally, brothers and sisters, whatever is true,
whatever is noble, whatever is right,
whatever is pure, whatever is lovely,
whatever is admirable
if anything is excellent or praiseworthy
think about such things.
Whatever you have learned or received
or heard from me or seen in me
put it into practice.
And the God of peace will be with you.*

Chapter 13: Remember that you are not just what you feel

Soon after the collapse of our bakery business, somebody close to us told me, "Why can't you seem to do anything right? Why do you keep making the same mistakes? When will you learn your lessons?"

That person meant well for me. She said those words out of concern, and that I was sure of. But unbeknownst to her, those words sent me spiraling further down into depression. It reverberated back to me a word that I was sure was me: failure. I felt that I had let so many people down, most especially my husband and two sons. I felt entirely responsible for why our costly attempt to put up a bakery business didn't work out. Even when I was aware of the many other aspects of why the business didn't work out, everything seemed to lead back to me: my decisions and my actions. I was the front man. My husband was working abroad, sending the money, but **I** made every crucial decision that mattered. It was all me. How could I have let everything fall apart?

Before all these happened, I had been a very confident person. I had done very well in school, got a lot of high marks and was generally admired and praised for what I produced. For many years, I was a youth leader in church and was respected by my peers. I was constantly approached by my friends for solutions to their problems. And most often, after a counselling session, they felt enlightened and certain of what they needed to do. I was regarded as a person who never wavered with my beliefs and principles, and someone who just knew what to do despite the odds. I was someone who settled for nothing, but the highest possible results.

How could I now be then so responsible for this mess? How could I be such a failure?

I had asked that question over and over all throughout my depression from December 2007 to December 2010. During the early months, I often thought of suicide each time I was hounded by that question. I just wanted so desperately to disappear from the face of the earth.

Little did I know what an amazing plan God had for me, and for my family. The meditation verse for this chapter could not have been more accurate for my life. God literally turned the mess that I created into His "**MESS**age". I may have done things that resulted in a disastrous financial burden for my family, but **failure was not what I was all about.** Rose Manalo is not **just** failure. I was so much more. And God knew that. The failures did not make up the entire journey. My failures, altogether, was simply part of the journey I was on.

I may have felt that it was the end of me. I may have felt crushed under the weight of my mistakes. But God, in His mighty power, everlasting wisdom and unending mercy towards me, was not in the least restricted by what "I felt". Instead, He shone His light on the next step of the journey, and then the next.

Fast forward to year 2017. I just received this text from one of our students: *"Rose, I want to thank you and Jet for teaching me and my husband how to bake breads and how to put up our own bakery business. Because of the training we had from you, we now have our own bakery here in our city. It is now earning enough that my husband has decided to stay and retire from his work abroad. We are now together as a family working with our kids at our bakery. Finally, the kids can be with their Dad and my husband can now be the doting father he had always wanted to be. We will be forever grateful to God and to you and Jet. May God bless you and strengthen you more, so you can help more families like mine."*

This is one of many similar messages of thanks we have received over the years from our students. And each time we receive one, we don't fail to feel at awe of God's mercy towards us and His amazing ways of turning what we see as complete mess into a powerful and meaningful MESSage that can benefit so many others.

Practical Guide:

1. Be and stay brave. You don't need to hide and avoid hearing things from people. They're not like the television which you can shut on or off, pause, or change channels. You can minimize your social contacts, but you shouldn't eliminate them altogether. That's not being practical or realistic. When I had finally crawled out of my depression pit, I was grateful for whatever social and blood relations I still have.

2. However, open your ears not just to what people say, but more so to what God says. What **HE** has to say is so much more important and TRUER than everything else.

He will tell you that you are **not just** all about what you feel.

But God...

Oh, how I wanted to just stop breathing
To escape this pain that's unrelenting
I've been reduced to mere nothing
I cannot see any reason to keep on going

But God who sees my suffering
Sees with eyes all-knowing
He sees past at what I'm staring
The pain and misery, onto the glorious ending

Genesis 50:20
Common English Bible (CEB)

*You planned something bad for me,
but God produced something good from it,
in order to save the lives of many people,
just as he's doing today.*

Job 42:2
New American Standard Bible (NASB)

*I know that You can do all things,
and that no purpose of Yours can be thwarted.*

Chapter 13: Realize that you are a work in progress

"The dough that died and lived again"
Part 1

One day, I was standing beside our dough mixer while the bread dough spun and stretched around the spiral hook of the machine. I was testing the newest bread recipe I had managed to formulate after several days of computations and re-computations. Since I didn't have that much of a budget for ingredients, I wanted desperately for this first batch to work, or at least to be not so far off the mark that I was trying to aim for.

Any minute now, it should be ready. A perfect dough should be warm to the touch, soft, pliant, and elastic. I decided to let another minute pass and then I pressed the off button. I reached down and dug my fingers into the dough to feel the temperature. I was shocked! It was too hot. I grabbed a portion and pulled it up and let go. It just slumped back onto the bottom of the mixing bowl without the spring and elasticity I expected it to have. My suspicion was confirmed: I had overheated the dough. Overheating is a direct result of overmixing. I should have not waited for that one last minute! How could I have been so careless! I knew better than to wait for another minute!

I beat myself up mentally and just stared and stared at the doughy mess I had just created. It's such a waste! What do I do now? If it was just a simple formula, I would not hesitate to throw it on a tray and let it rise and then bake and turn it into bread crumbs. At least, it would have had some sort of redemption and purpose.

But this one is an extra special, more expensive formulation. I had intended it to produce very soft breads that will stay soft for many more hours. I touched and squeezed the dough again and again, and I kept arriving to the same conclusion. It was too overmixed and too soft. Therefore, it cannot hold enough air during proofing time, and it will surely deflate which will then result in flat, airless, hard breads. It was definitely far off the mark. It is time to turn it into an "extra special, more expensive" bread crumbs.

I was still shaking my head and feeling so disappointed as I reached down to pull all the dough out of the mixer, when all of a sudden, I thought of adding more flour, or maybe more water? What if I can still save this dough and turn it to another kind of breads? My mind juggled all the ingredients in my head, trying to figure out how much to add for which ingredient.

I carefully weighed all the ingredients that I decided to add making sure I took note of each. I then turned the mixer on again and then added the extra ingredients. After a few minutes, my perseverance was rewarded with a kind of dough that was silky smooth, yet strong and pliable. I hurriedly portioned and weighed each piece and shaped them. I could hardly wait for the proofing time to finish its job.

After the proofing time was done and the dough didn't deflate after reaching its maximum size, I let myself smile, although the process wasn't finished yet. I crossed my fingers and hoped that the dough could hold its shape during the baking time. If my calculations were correct, the dough, during the first few minutes of baking should freely give way to "oven spring" when it will further expand before its crust hardens as it bakes in the intense heat. I made sure that the oven had the perfect temperature and then I slid the tray in and closed the oven door. It will need just under 15 minutes of baking time, but I will let the smell of the baking bread and finally the color of the crust decide its doneness.

At 12 minutes, the aroma from the oven started to change, and so I cracked open the oven door slightly and peeped inside. The top still lacked the color I wanted, so I closed the oven door again. Finally, right before reaching 15 minutes, I opened the door and slid the tray out and laid it on the table. In front of me was a tray of the most amazing-looking brioche buns. Here, we call it "ensaymada".

For the next 6 parts of this same chapter title, together we will scrutinize every step of the mixing and baking process I have just written above, as it relates to our life. For now, let me tell you that **God is not done with you**, just as He wasn't done with me and just as I wasn't done with my "seemingly dead" dough.

Practical Guide:

1. Read the meditation verse at least 7 times. Read it slower and slower each time. One of those times I was reading this verse, I just stared at the word "know". God **knows** His plans for me. I can just stop right there. God knows His plans for me. God knows his plans for **you**. How does that make you feel? The God of the universe, the God who created the heavens and the earth, and who created you, **knows** His plans for you!

2. Another word from this verse that I truly sunk my teeth into is "hope". I realize that it's the totally hopeless that can benefit the most from receiving hope.

3. You need to "ruminate" on God's Word. If there was one practical exercise I did that I benefitted the most for every aspect of my being, it was **ruminating** on the Word of God. It says in Joshua 1:8 to "Keep this Book of the Law always on your lips; meditate on it day and night, so that you may be careful to do everything written in it. Then you will be prosperous and successful." The word "meditate" means to "ruminate". Among all the definitions I've looked up on ruminate, I particularly liked the one from Vocabulary.com (https://www.vocabulary.com/ dictionary/ruminate):

    - When you ruminate, it means you are thinking very deeply about something. You're likely to be so lost in thought that you stare off into space and don't hear people when they call your name.

    - Another meaning of ruminate is to "chew the cud," which can mean "to turn it over and over in your mind." Or, if you're a cow, to turn food over and over in your stomachs in order to digest it. Whether you're a human or a cow, if you ruminate, it will take a LONG time.

I guess what made this exercise of rumination easier for me to do was my introverted personality. I just kept to myself and had so much time in my hands, although this can be either beneficial or damaging. However, the calming effect of God's Word on me was so "physical" that I felt it immediately each time I exposed myself to the Word. I felt relieved and relaxed each time I was reading the Word of God (or through Christian cable or online programs). Hence, spending many hours studying the Word and ruminating on it became not just a way for me to pass the time, but it also enabled me to convert what could easily be basking in my depression and grumbling in a corner, into a glorious opening for me to be relieved of constant pain and suffering.

4. The Amplified Bible translation of Jeremiah 29:11 used the word "disaster". My dough seemed like a disaster. Your life may seem like one to you right now. My life indeed seemed hopeless and lifeless, but God turned it around. You know why? Because He never meant for me to be a disaster, to be hopeless and lifeless. Just like I never meant for my dough to end up a disaster. I did everything I could to turn it around **and it resurrected into something far better than I first intended.**

Truly my life was like the dough that died and lived again because I was a work **still** in progress.

Pain Remixed

It's difficult to feel other than pain
Hearing nothing but blame again and again
Seeing faces filled with disdain
Shackling me tighter in depressive chain

But God ruled in His domain
In it I belonged and so's all my agonizing pain
He stirred, mixed and turned them into gain
I emerged with a purpose, without even a stain

Jeremiah 29:11
New International Version (NIV)

"For I know the plans I have for you", declares the Lord,
"plans to prosper you and not to harm you,
plans to give you hope and a future".

Jeremiah 29:11
Amplified Bible (AMP)

"For I know the plans and thoughts that I have for you",
says the Lord, "plans for peace and well-being
and not for disaster, to give you a future and a hope".

Chapter 14: Learn to shrug it off

We have a saying in Filipino that goes like this *"Ang pikon, talo."* In English it means *"a man who has lost his temper is a loser"*. I have my own translation for this saying and it goes like this, *"you don't gain anything by being easily offended."*

I am proud to say that its personal meaning is born out of years of being easily offended by people around me. Someone once told me, a person that's easily offended can be compared to a pus-filled wound: it aches at the slightest touch.

After years of letting myself be easily offended, I have come to realize that there's nothing about it that nurtured my soul. None at all! After each episode of my "feeling offended", I felt exhausted. I was even more disgusted, not at the person who offended me, but at myself.

An experience while driving along the highway paved the way for me to start 'wanting' to be much less sensitive and be more forgiving and understanding. I was driving at the appropriate speed at the inner lane. Suddenly, a car came up behind me at a dangerously close distance and started honking repeatedly. I felt my blood rising quickly to my face and my heart palpitating even faster. I gripped the stirring wheel harder and resolutely kept my speed and stayed in my lane. I was fuming and my kids at the back were looking at my face. Then the car skidded to the left lane and as it overtook us, my son saw that the passenger at the back was hunched over beside a woman who looked heavily pregnant. My son explained to me what he saw, and I felt like a cold gush of water was poured over me and all of a sudden, the anger disappeared. I felt calm, but exhausted. And yes, I had that feeling of disgust toward myself. Then a mental picture of that lady in the car, who probably was in labor and about to give birth, came into my mind. I found myself saying a prayer for her and her family. Next, I asked for God's forgiveness for failing to help a person in need because I chose to take offense instead.

Ever since that day, those two elements of prayer (praying for the source of offense, and for forgiveness for taking offense) have been effective for me in avoiding taking offense. And eventually I have learned how to immediately shrug off an offense. Just shake it off!

Practical Guide:

1. Take your daily dosage of Niacin flush-free (Vit. B3) and eat foods rich in healthy fats like butter, eggs, bacon, and fatty fish like salmon and mackerel. I wrote in my first book why these foods are crucial for healing from depression.

2. Should you succeed in keeping your anger in check, after an offense, the next thing you will most likely feel is that strong desire to "mull" it over. Before you know it, you are "unfriending" that person, or concocting a plan to get even. Proverbs 12:16 offers a quick solution: ignore it. When you ignore an insult, you don't think about it and you don't mull over it. I admit though that some offenses can push some of our nastiest buttons. And in my experience, a quick prayer of forgiveness is the best deterrent that has stopped me in my tracks over and over again. Here's mine: *"Father, I feel offended by (name of person). Help me get over this offense and heal my heart. Please take care of (name of person)."*

It's **not worth** your precious, limited energy. So, learn to shrug it off.

Do nothing

Shoo! I am not giving in to you
Not this time, no way! Yahoo!

You, pus-filled-easily-irked sensitive lump
Of vibrating anger with nothing but grump

You're the most unpleasant, belligerent bug
No one should mind you, you ought to be fogged

Better yet, flogged and brought to submission
To steal your chance of making me your minion

Have had enough of you and all misery you bring
You made "getting back" so justified and inviting

Yet all it's done to me all these senseless years
Wasn't promised pleasures but multiplied my fears

While in your grasp that seemed to tighten even more
Each time I convulsed with you in such passionate furor

Now here is my precious chance to finally be set free
From your tight grip, so viciously sticky

Get this: I will relax and refuse to give in to the urge
I will stay this way, breathe easy and not let it resurge

I will center on this sensation that is simply liberating
As I surrender to doing just plain.....nothing

Proverbs 12:16
Amplified Bible (AMP)

*The [arrogant] fool's anger is quickly known
[because he lacks self-control and common sense],
But a prudent man ignores an insult.*

Proverbs 29:11
Common English Bible (CEB)

*Fools show all their anger,
but the wise hold it back.*

Chapter 15: Cool down your overheated spirit

"The dough that died and lived again"
Part 2

When we had to close our bakery business, I began my 3-year depression. Too many things were going on at the same time. Every day I received at least four phone calls from people we owed money to in some shape or form.

One time, I had received a call from our bank, and they informed me that our check had bounced. I phoned the person to whom I issued the check and pleaded with her not to redeposit our check until such date that I was sure I had enough funds for the check. She refused. She said she would redeposit the check as soon as possible, and that I had better make sure that it was funded. That whole day I felt sick in my stomach. I just found myself staring into nothingness not knowing what to do. I was over-heating.

Prior to all these, I've never faced anything like this. I've never had to beg anyone like I begged that lady about the check. I've never had to juggle so many concerns of different nature and at different levels. I've never had to do it all at the same time, and I have never had to do it all alone. My husband, Jet, during this time, was still working abroad. All I had were our two sons, then aged 13 and 10. I kept thinking about them, and their well-being was constantly in my mind.

Several weeks into depression, I felt lifeless and very weak, like a spineless jelly. It's like I was there, and yet I had no bones to support myself. In the house, I would get up and walk from one area to another and I wouldn't remember using my legs to do it. It felt like I was just floating. But what gave me so much more dread was what I felt in my chest. There was always a sharp pain right in the middle. I didn't know which was better: that perpetual sharp pain in my chest or the weakness in my limbs.

When a dough overheats, there is only one reason. It is overmixed. An overheated dough is often stale, lifeless, not pliable at all, and when stretched, it will not bounce back. It will just lay flat down when released. An overheated dough cannot be shaped properly because it's not stretchable or pliable. For as long as it is overheated, the dough cannot be used.

For most times that I had to revive a lifeless overheated dough, I always had to do two things immediately: give it time to cool down and then splash it with a little water.

I thank God that He knew exactly what He needed to do with His overheated dough: me. He gave me time to cool down and He gave me His Word, the divine water. He knew every ingredient that went into this dough. He knew everything that caused my overheating and He knew exactly how to fix and revive me and make me useful again.

Practical Guide:

1. Give God a chance. Just give Him a chance. Let Him splash you down with His Word. Read it and wait for it to take its effect on you. The Word of God's immediate effect on me was peace. There was turmoil in my heart, and the dread was still there. I still felt weak and terrified and fearful every waking minute, but now there was peace. The peace didn't drive these other things away, but again there was peace. It was a welcome feeling, almost like a sensation. Like what that dough must have felt. I felt immediately cooled down whenever I was exposed to the Word of God.

2. Try this daily devotional site: Joyce Meyer Ministries (http://www.joycemeyer.org/Articles/Devotional.aspx)

Let God's Word **cool down** your overheated spirit.

64

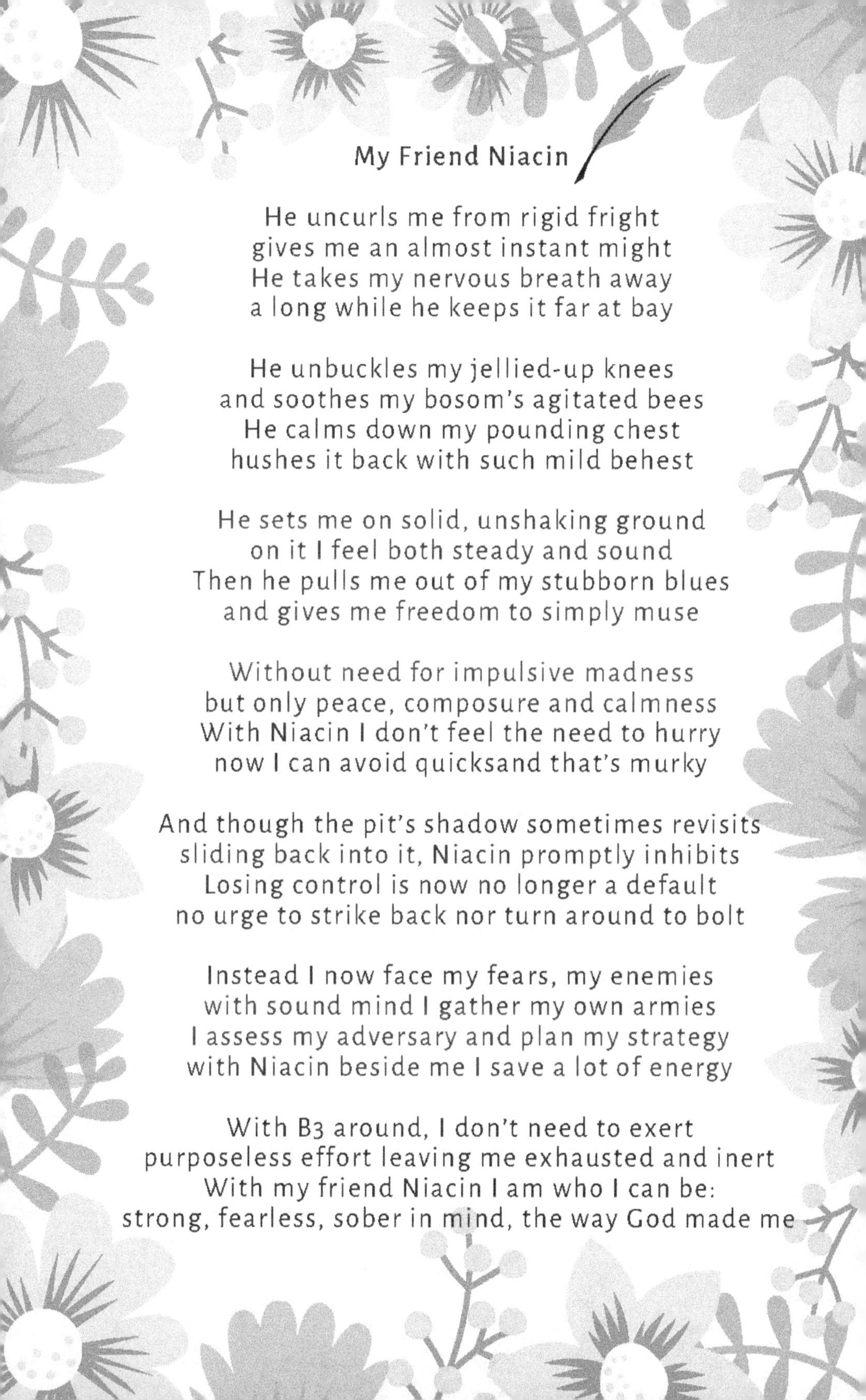

My Friend Niacin

He uncurls me from rigid fright
gives me an almost instant might
He takes my nervous breath away
a long while he keeps it far at bay

He unbuckles my jellied-up knees
and soothes my bosom's agitated bees
He calms down my pounding chest
hushes it back with such mild behest

He sets me on solid, unshaking ground
on it I feel both steady and sound
Then he pulls me out of my stubborn blues
and gives me freedom to simply muse

Without need for impulsive madness
but only peace, composure and calmness
With Niacin I don't feel the need to hurry
now I can avoid quicksand that's murky

And though the pit's shadow sometimes revisits
sliding back into it, Niacin promptly inhibits
Losing control is now no longer a default
no urge to strike back nor turn around to bolt

Instead I now face my fears, my enemies
with sound mind I gather my own armies
I assess my adversary and plan my strategy
with Niacin beside me I save a lot of energy

With B3 around, I don't need to exert
purposeless effort leaving me exhausted and inert
With my friend Niacin I am who I can be:
strong, fearless, sober in mind, the way God made me

Psalm 119:28
New International Version (NIV)

*My soul is weary with sorrow;
strengthen me according to your word.*

Psalm 119:130
Amplified Bible (AMP)

*The unfolding of Your [glorious] words gives light;
their unfolding gives understanding to the simple
(childlike).*

Chapter 16: Get to know your own yoke, then hate it

During my depressed years, there were so many times that I felt so alone and sad with a heavy heart. But then after moments of praying for God's presence and help, that feeling of heaviness, sadness and being alone, would start fading.

One day, I was sitting at my study, meditating and having just said that prayer. And there it was again: I felt that sudden lift in my spirit, though there was still a tinge of burden. Soon after, I had an epiphany that explained it all. The heaviness, sadness and loneliness didn't actually leave. However, this time, I'm carrying them with another Person's help. I was carrying them with Jesus. He was there because I asked for Him. Everything became clear: I was walking with a common yoke over both our necks. He was carrying as much weight as I was carrying, but only half of the total weight.

Then I remembered Matthew 11:28-30 *"Come to Me, all who are weary and heavy-laden, and I will give you rest. Take My yoke upon you and learn from Me, for I am gentle and humble in heart, and you will find rest for your souls. For My yoke is easy and My burden is light."*

I told God *"Lord, you said your yoke is easy and light. But why do I feel this way? When will I stop feeling so much terrifying fear, sadness, and all these weakness in my limbs?"* Even before I finished my question, I felt the answer in my spirit. I wasn't carrying God's yoke. I was carrying **my** yoke; the yoke that I made myself. It was heavy, because it was made of pride, self-will, stubbornness, selfishness, everything that God isn't. I cannot carry two yokes at the same time. I need to be willing to let go of my own yoke and then "learn" from Jesus about humility and gentleness, the stuff His yoke is made of.

During those dark times, God was letting me get fully acquainted with my own yoke. Yes, He was helping me carry it, but not all of it because I might forget that awful feeling of carrying it. I once heard a preacher say, *"you cannot really be free from sin until you've learned to hate it"*. I am now feeling the full weight of the consequences of being prideful, hasty, and selfish. I must navigate my way out of this mess. If the Lord would just miraculously pluck me out of my misery, I would just simply find my way back. I knew that for certain because I knew myself well. But most importantly, God knew me. He knew how much I could handle, and He knew just what was needed for me to learn my lessons.

Practical Guide:

Make a journal. Write down as much as you can get from your daily devotions. After a few weeks, take time to open and read your early entries. I assure you that you would be surprised by how far you've gone in terms of faith, trust, and even thoughts and behavior. God has a purpose for you, and He started working the very day you asked Him to take over. No matter how bad you feel about yourself and your mistakes today, take comfort in facts. Your journal won't lie. It will show you where you've been and where you are now.

Get to know your own yoke, but **don't get too comfortable** under it. Learn to hate it.

There's more to letting go

I never thought I'd see the day
"Goodbye" to you I'd have to say
You've been such a part of me
More than I was willing to set free

Couldn't imagine any life without
Because I have had you always about
You were never ever not here
Through pain, laughter, easy or severe

Through bad, better, good and best
Having you I felt I couldn't be more blest
'til one day the most excellent came into view
Everything you've got suddenly was too few

What used to be sufficient and enough
Now could not even reach a decent half
What to do now other than reconsider
The possibility that there's someone far better

On and on and on I clung to you to stay
Couldn't accept 'twas time for the worthier mainstay
No matter how much I try to deny
Your reliable well has finally run dry

I cannot see it yet I cannot prove it yet
This wonderful other I have yet to beget
For now, deep in me I'm sure, I know
there is so much more to letting you go

1 Thessalonians 5:21-28
New American Standard Bible (NASB)

But examine everything carefully;
hold fast to that which is good;
abstain from every form of evil.
Now may the God of peace Himself
sanctify you entirely;
and may your spirit and soul and body
be preserved complete,
without blame
at the coming of our Lord Jesus Christ.
Faithful is He who calls you,
and He also will bring it to pass.

Chapter 17: Suck it in

"The dough that died and lived again"
Part 3

An overheated dough has to be given time to cool down. Just a few minutes will suffice. When touched and it's not "burning" anymore, it is comparable to a person's skin with slight fever.

The next step then is to revive it; splash it down with a bit of cold water. Sprinkle here and there. Then turn on the mixer again to incorporate the water into the dough to further bring down its internal temperature. The water won't work its job until it is slowly incorporated into the dough through the mixing action.

The Word of God didn't start doing its job in my spirit until I started reading it and rereading it over and over again. Reading a passage just one time made it seem vague and foreign. I borrowed my brother's Bible Concordance and that changed everything for me. I looked up in the concordance every word that didn't make sense to me in the Bible passage. Reading the Bible with the help of the concordance was like looking at a coloring book page that suddenly had the right bright colors it needed.

I made it a habit not to loosely jump from one scripture to the next without first thoroughly understanding the previous one. Just like an overheated dough, I could feel I was drowning in water when I was reading too much scripture too soon. Take it easy. Ruminate on each passage. Let it sink in. Let it douse you with understanding.

Take for example John 1:14. After meditating on this short passage and understanding the meaning of Jesus being full of "grace" and "truth", my heart was enveloped in peace. At that time, I had a lot of deceptions in my life. As soon as I started getting exposed to the Word, I sensed in my spirit a gentle but definite stirring. Just like the dough, I was being stretched, and pushed and squeezed and twisted in all sorts of directions. The **truth** in the Word exposed one at a time every lie in my life, including some so-called friends that don't really mean well for me. And in a smaller radius, my character and personality. Just when I was starting to feel vulnerable, condemned, dirty and underserving, the **grace** of God took over, and it was like a healing balm to my cracked and dry soul.

To help me understand further, I read "commentaries" just on this particular passage. Back in 2008 to 2009, I had to flip through very thick books and read very small texts. These days, you can just "google" a passage and instantly the wealth of information is right there on your computer screen, though the varied websites on this can easily overwhelm you. Pay close attention to the practical tips I gave below.

Practical Guide:

1. These two Bible websites are my favorites:
    a. Biblegateway.com (https://www.biblegateway.com/)
    b. Biblehub.com (http://biblehub.com/commentaries/ jeremiah/15-16.htm)
    You may also download their app on your smartphone.
2. Be careful not to get yourself overwhelmed. That is why it pays to ruminate on a smaller passage than the whole chapter in one sitting. I do however encourage you to try to understand the whole context. But personally, after reading the whole chapter, I find it manageable and just as rewarding to meditate on smaller passages, *in order* to give me a wider and clearer perspective.

Delight your soul in God's Word and let it cool you down. **Suck it in.**

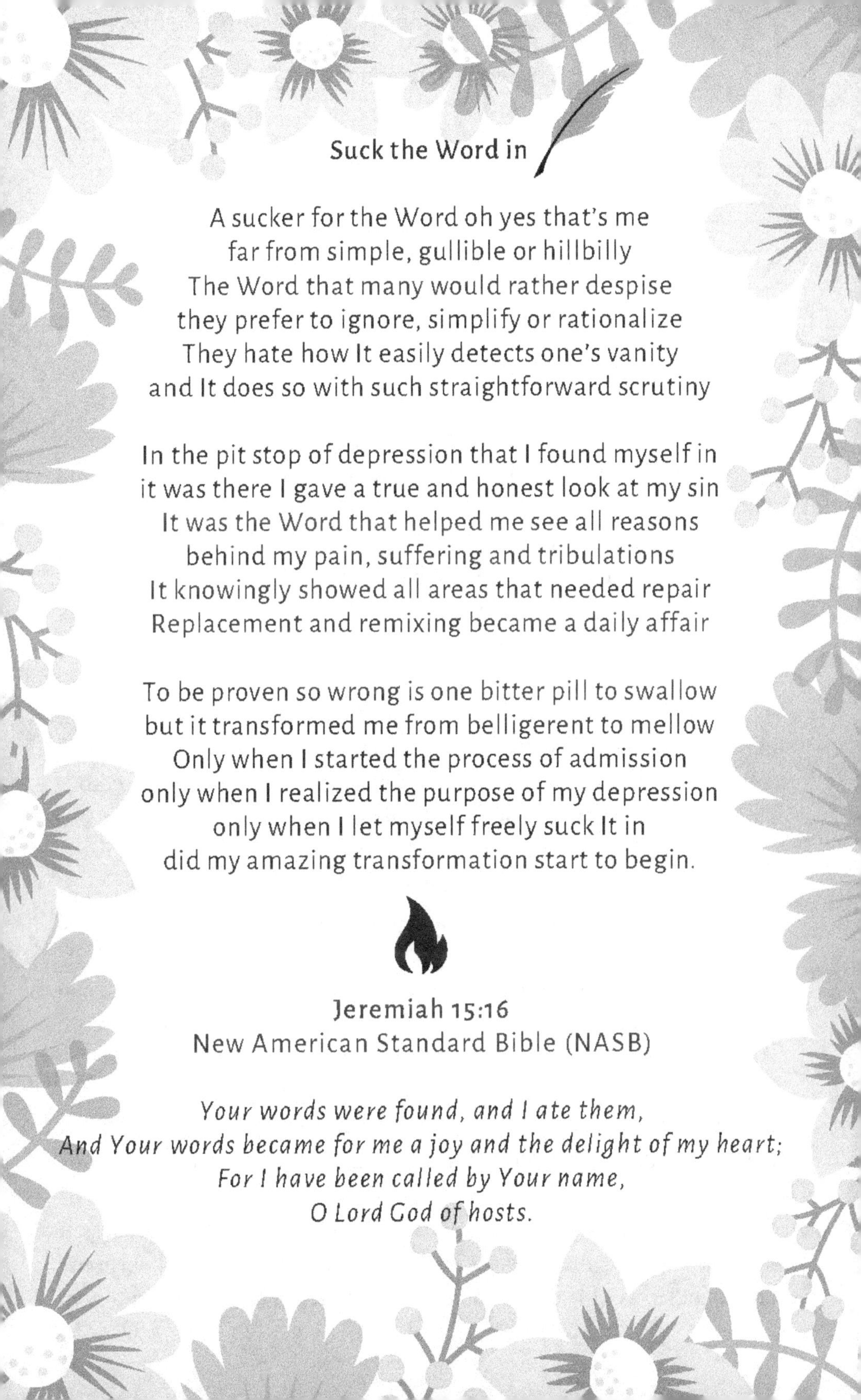

Suck the Word in

A sucker for the Word oh yes that's me
far from simple, gullible or hillbilly
The Word that many would rather despise
they prefer to ignore, simplify or rationalize
They hate how It easily detects one's vanity
and It does so with such straightforward scrutiny

In the pit stop of depression that I found myself in
it was there I gave a true and honest look at my sin
It was the Word that helped me see all reasons
behind my pain, suffering and tribulations
It knowingly showed all areas that needed repair
Replacement and remixing became a daily affair

To be proven so wrong is one bitter pill to swallow
but it transformed me from belligerent to mellow
Only when I started the process of admission
only when I realized the purpose of my depression
only when I let myself freely suck It in
did my amazing transformation start to begin.

Jeremiah 15:16
New American Standard Bible (NASB)

Your words were found, and I ate them,
And Your words became for me a joy and the delight of my heart;
For I have been called by Your name,
O Lord God of hosts.

Chapter 18: Forgive and cover

In Chapter 3, I discussed the initial process of forgiveness through the mouth by abstaining from talking about the people who have offended you or caused you harm. This practice has had a dual effect in my life: it has stopped additional negativity and has promoted an atmosphere where blessings can thrive. Soon after I decided to stop talking about the people who have hurt us, opportunities to do so came to a stop as well. I had learned to resist the temptation as I kept on refusing to engage in the practice.

Among other factors, it had helped enhance the soil out of which blessings sprouted. Our bakery teaching business grew exponentially and expanded in ways I didn't even think possible. It had released our family from the shackles of financial debts, enabled us to purchase our own house (after 23 years of marriage and 15 house transfers), enjoy the simple pleasures of family life, and extend help to others as well.

In this therapy chapter, we are going to go deeper into the process of forgiveness: **covering**.

Peace and harmony between you and your past, present and future relations, or the lack of it, can either help re-open or keep close the lid on your pit of depression. Understanding this extra step into the process of forgiveness will make the act of forgiving so much easier to do and to stay true to its essence. This step is vital not only to get you out of your depression pit, but also to make sure you don't slide back into it.

As soon as I had decided to walk on the path of forgiveness, I became aware of the constant struggle to stay on it. One opportunity after another would surface, and this would temp me to give in to that itchy desire to strike back, defend myself, and clear my name or to just try to "balance" the way people regarded "my side of the story". I soon realized that I couldn't avoid the trap of slander since it was an inevitable consequence of my efforts to redeem my name.

However, when I finally understood that I couldn't enjoy one without the other, I decided to drop both. I then realized it's far easier to just keep quiet when I am not giving in to the "itch" of grabbing every opportunity to clear my name.

I was on that road for about three years when something more started happening.

One day I found myself being challenged to "cover" those who have offended, maligned and hurt us.

It was the first day of one of our bread baking training sessions when one of our students said, *"You know that popular bakery at the market, they have very lousy breads!"*.

I asked for the name of the bakery and it was the one owned by our "nemesis", our former franchisor. Another student butted in, *"I heard that that's the bakery offering franchises in this area."*

A couple more minutes passed and within that period, each time the bakery's name was mentioned, it seemed like a delicious bait to grab the chance and satisfy the old cantankerous me.

I would have preferred to just keep quiet because that's what had kept me from falling into the "slander trap", but then much to my surprise, I heard myself say, *"Are you sure? I mean about their breads? Because I used to buy from them regularly, and I was always satisfied with the quality of their breads."*

What was surprising to me was that my words were positive and that I meant every word because that was the truth. Their bakery produced high quality breads and they have been consistent over the years.

Seconds after sensing relief that I had passed this "new challenge", a fresh one came, in the form of another question by the student who spoke about the franchise. *"If they offer quality breads, how come their last franchise in the other city closed down?"*, she asked.

I took time to consider my answer and then I said, *"Well, maybe it could be many other reasons. Like in our case, I knew so little about franchising. I dove right into something I didn't have enough knowledge of. There was very little research and preparation on my part. I relied 100% on our franchisors who, themselves, were new in the field. It could be that, you know, or something else. Maybe the chosen area wasn't ideal. But one thing I'm sure of, it cannot be because of poor quality breads, unless they had similar problems as we did with the premixes we ordered from our franchisor."*

(Please note that the students involved in this conversation were not aware of the identity of our franchisors, it is a piece of information that my husband and I have decided long before, not to disclose to our students, should they have asked.)

The student who spoke negatively about the breads was suddenly quiet and offered no further comments. Could it be that she was just out to malign this bakery's owners and their business? If she was, then I not only passed my own test, but I had even managed to stop her in her tracks, or at the least, douse her intentions.

In bed that evening, the scene kept replaying in my head in a loop. "What was new this time?", I asked myself. What ingredient was added into the mix that made this bitter pill of forgiveness much easier to swallow, this time around?

The answer came in a remembrance of a Proverb:

Proverbs 20:3 New American Standard Bible (NASB)

"Keeping away from strife is an honor for a man,
But any fool will quarrel."

That was it. That pleasant sensation I felt was spiritual. It was **honor**. I felt the first trickles of this sensation the moment I restrained myself from bursting out a vindictive remark and chose instead to mull over my reply. The effect was amazingly comforting, even in its smallest dose. Something was assuring me and whispering, *"You're on the right track. Stay on it."*

The Bible uses another word that's similar to *"keeping away from strife"*, and that is the word *"cover"*. We see this word in this translation of Proverbs 10:12,

(English Standard Version) *"Hatred stirs up strife, but love **covers** all offenses."*

And in the Contemporary English Version of the same verse, we see the word *"overlook"* in place of *"cover"*:

Proverbs 10:12 Contemporary English Version (CEV)

*"Hatred stirs up trouble; love **overlooks** the wrongs that others do."*

When I subtly declined to take part in my student's criticism of our adversary, I started the process of covering. And when I let my mouth say those words that provided balance to their skewed perception of the subject, I completed the process of covering. I helped others to step back, overlook the negative, and consider the bigger, and more complete picture.

However, I held fast to my equally important resolve to help my students make sound decisions with regard to putting up their own bakery business. Up to this day, Jet and I untiringly explain to them the pros and cons of bakery franchises and how owning their own independent, franchise-free bakery trumps that of a franchised one. We present the plain facts surrounding the collapse of our own franchised bakery, including our own mistakes. We do all these without engaging in malicious conversation, careful to focus on the circumstances and not on the personalities.

One might say that the challenges I have faced as a victim of offence is somewhat on the lower side of the spectrum of hurt and suffering. In comparison to those who have suffered unimaginable horror and agony in the hands of others, my efforts to "forgive and cover" may seem so insignificant. But here's the thing: in the middle of a battle, we perceive our problems through our own eyes and not through others. We assess our difficulties in view of our abilities to overcome them. A rich man who has lost all his possessions might feel equally distressed as a poor man who had lost his one and only cloak.

Those three anxiety-riddled depression years had almost pushed me over into the depths of insanity. Today, as my lips continually utter praises of thanks to God for my deliverance, each one is always coupled with a plea for Him to keep me and my family from anything beyond we are able to bear. And these pleadings are perpetual reminders for me to stay humble and forgiving, as they don't fail to evoke in me the agony I went through.

Practical Guide:

1. Do not hesitate to pray for those who have hurt you and even for those who continually repay your goodness with evil. God knows what He's doing, and He is their Father as He is yours. What makes us recoil from praying for our enemies is the prospect that God would simply ignore their offenses and shower them with blessings instead. God doesn't work that way, based on how I have seen Him work in my life and those around me. He is a God who always has the best possible end-result in mind for His children, but that end-result may go through different stages of development. He tailor-fits each process and makes sure the person comes out "changed". Having seen God at work several times with others, and ever mindful of my own journey inside each process, I have become acquainted with one factor that inevitably determines how long the process becomes, and that is humility. Hence, I have learned how to word my prayer for those who have hurt me:

   "Father I pray for _________. May You give them the grace of humility as they go through their process of change."

2. When the pain is too fresh and is preventing you from uttering the prayer, this "pre-prayer" will help:

   "Father, please help me pray the prayer. Help me start forgiving."

   At times, it may take a while before you experience a change of heart. Stay patient. God is at work using His own timeline, not ours.

3. Remember that from the time I stopped talking about our enemies to the time I found the grace to "cover" them was a significant period. It was probably 2 to 3 years of regular testing. Do not attempt to skip a process. Stay true to each change. Nourish it well until you don't feel any struggle anymore. The words that flowed out of me in the story above were effortless. And since it was time for the "level-up", when I spoke those words, they blessed me as well as those who heard them.

4. If you find yourself falling into the vengeance trap, remember Therapy Session Chapter 5: Sulk if You Must. Ponder the whys of how you were not able to avoid the trap. I have learned to appreciate these times of mulling over my failings and I do so almost in a forensic way, looking at every angle, even at my physiological state at the time. I analyze the reasons by way of asking some questions: Have I been neglecting my supplements, most especially Vitamin B3? Is it that time of the month? (monthly period). Have I been getting enough rest and sleep? Did I have too much coffee? Was I bothered by something else? Have I been neglecting my prayer time? Have I been neglecting the health of my gut (I wrote in my first book about importance of our second brain: our GUT)?

   In more than one occasion I gave in to the urge to take offense and went down the path of slander, speaking degrading words about my detractors. As soon as I started my "regret session" I knew what caused my weakness. It was the week before my period which enhanced my susceptibility to being emotional. But what made me a more willing victim was the fact that I was neglecting my supplements.

5. Lessen your associations with people who love to gossip. Push them out of your circle. Staying away from gossipers, as far as possible, is the only way for you to see clearly a gossip's true color. In all those instances when I fell into the trap of vengeance and slander, I was always in the company of one. Until you are iron-clad in your resolve to forgive and cover, stay clear of a gossip's shadow.

Forgiveness is **complete** once you are willing to cover the offense.

Love for Pain for Love

You knocked on my door, cheeks wet with tears
You needed a lot of help, heart enveloped in fears
Your bones were sharp lines beneath your skin
Your last meal, how long has it been?

I opened my arms and extended my hand
Listened to your woes careful not to misunderstand
I stayed beside you until you felt at ease
Kept you from anything that will disturb your peace

In a very short while you became strong
And stronger still after not very long
Your bones now hidden under a healthy layer of fat
You can now smile and even carry on a chat

Then one day you said you wanted to venture out
To try and see if you're strong enough to go about
Found a bigger door on which you knocked and knocked
Never returned for a proper goodbye, I was gobsmacked!

From behind the big door wind swept some words back
Words far from gratitude but more like an attack
on my name and what we have done for you in our care
was so untrue, my heart was crushed, it was all so unfair!

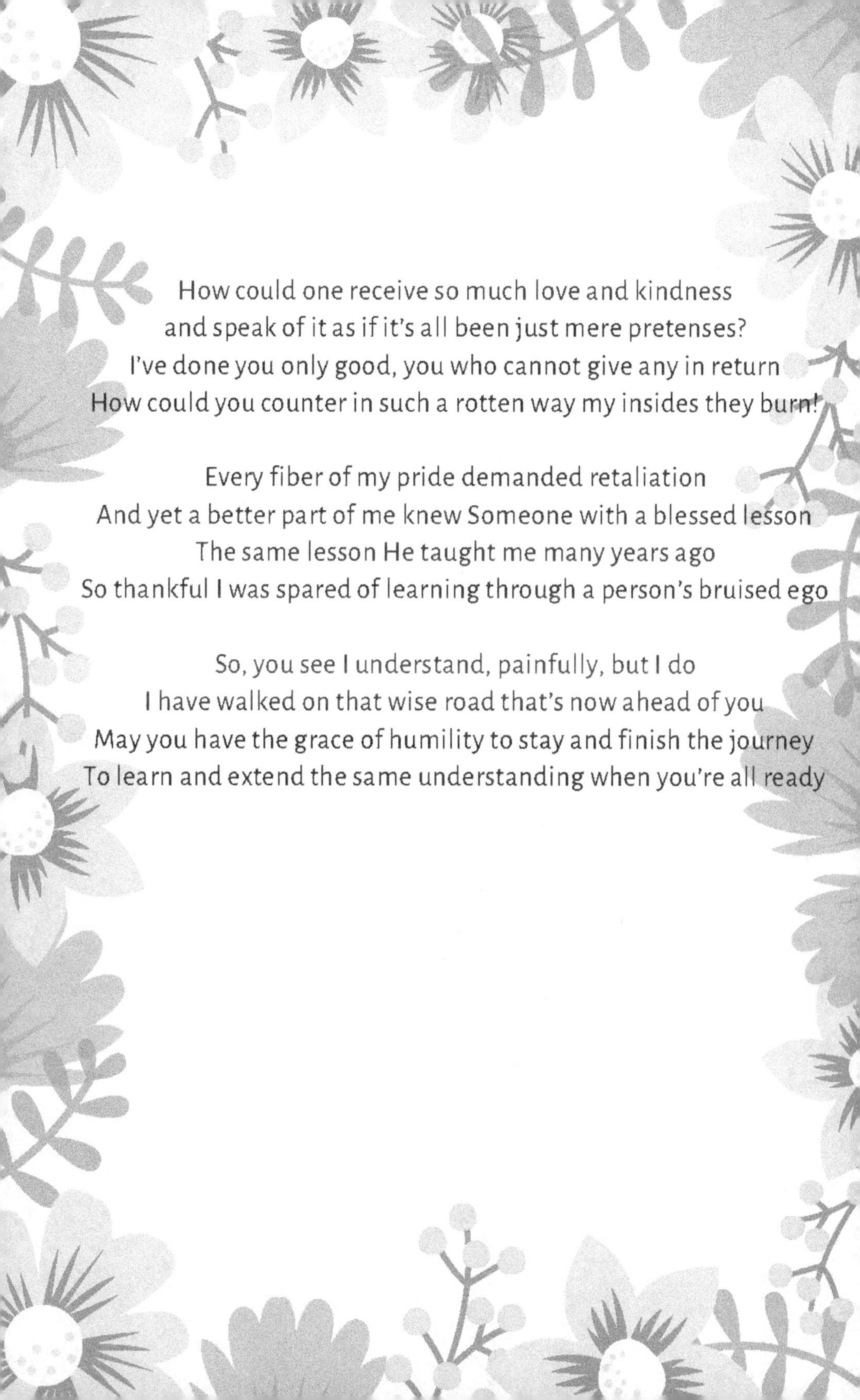

How could one receive so much love and kindness
and speak of it as if it's all been just mere pretenses?
I've done you only good, you who cannot give any in return
How could you counter in such a rotten way my insides they burn!

Every fiber of my pride demanded retaliation
And yet a better part of me knew Someone with a blessed lesson
The same lesson He taught me many years ago
So thankful I was spared of learning through a person's bruised ego

So, you see I understand, painfully, but I do
I have walked on that wise road that's now ahead of you
May you have the grace of humility to stay and finish the journey
To learn and extend the same understanding when you're all ready

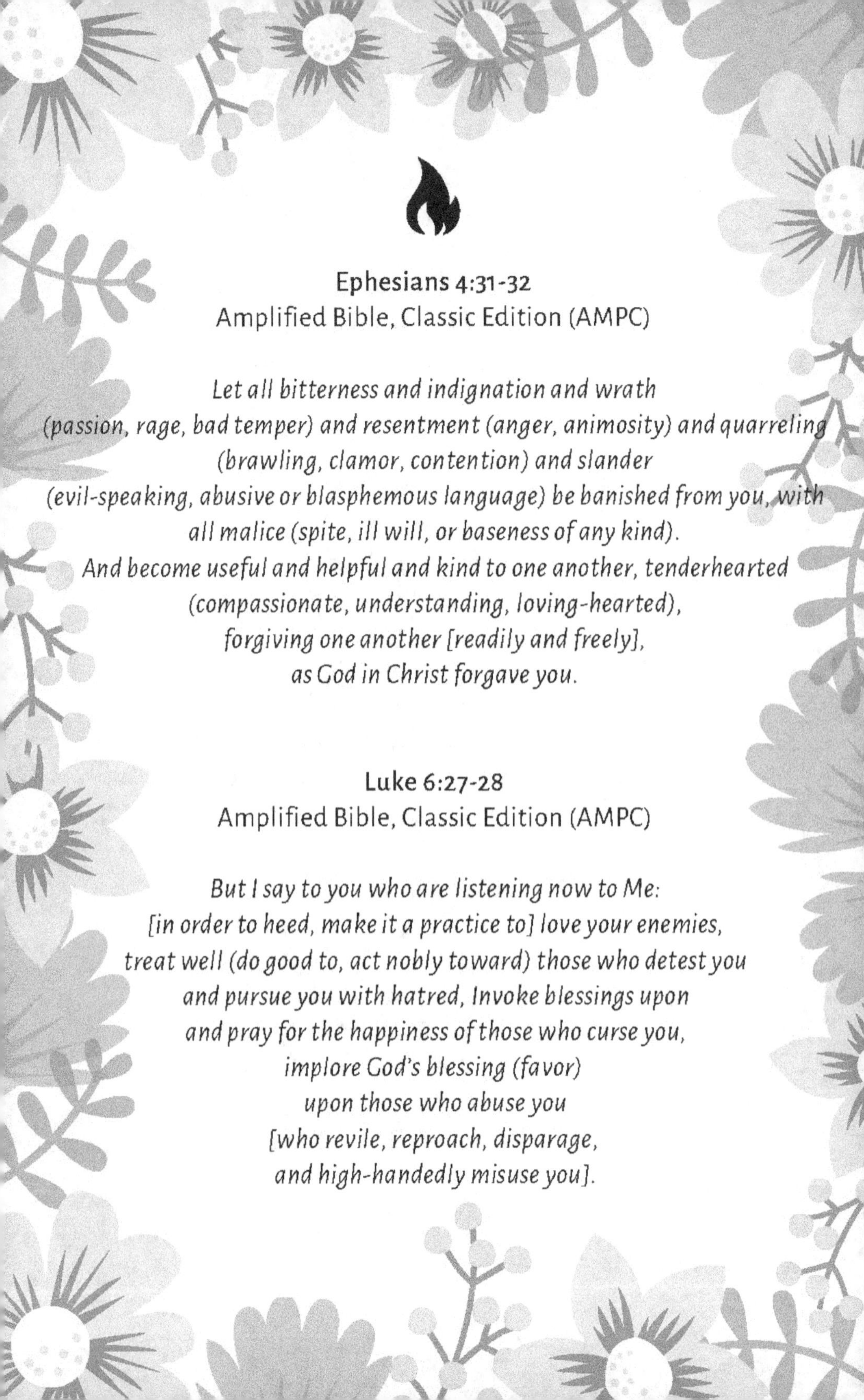

Ephesians 4:31-32
Amplified Bible, Classic Edition (AMPC)

Let all bitterness and indignation and wrath
(passion, rage, bad temper) and resentment (anger, animosity) and quarreling
(brawling, clamor, contention) and slander
(evil-speaking, abusive or blasphemous language) be banished from you, with
all malice (spite, ill will, or baseness of any kind).
And become useful and helpful and kind to one another, tenderhearted
(compassionate, understanding, loving-hearted),
forgiving one another [readily and freely],
as God in Christ forgave you.

Luke 6:27-28
Amplified Bible, Classic Edition (AMPC)

But I say to you who are listening now to Me:
[in order to heed, make it a practice to] love your enemies,
treat well (do good to, act nobly toward) those who detest you
and pursue you with hatred, Invoke blessings upon
and pray for the happiness of those who curse you,
implore God's blessing (favor)
upon those who abuse you
[who revile, reproach, disparage,
and high-handedly misuse you].

Chapter 19: Brace yourself to be remixed

"The dough that died and lived again"
Part 4

The purpose of the whole process of reviving a dead dough is to bring it back up to a level where it can be useful again. First, it entails that the baker should be able to shape it in whatever way he wants. During proofing, the dough should be able to keep air and rise without deflating. It should be able to withstand the intense heat of the oven, where it bursts into its final shape and form and stay that way, until it is bought and eaten by the customer.

However, before all that is even possible, the dough, after it has cooled down, has to be remixed with some more of its original ingredients. The baker will determine the exact amount of flour he needs to add. It may be a little more yeast, sugar, salt, or oil. It all depends on how the baker analyzes the dough by its feel and visual condition. He also will have to consider whether he aims for a different "finish" for the dough or he still takes a shot for his original plan.

For all the occasions that I had to revive a dead dough, a revived one always turned out different from the "original" plan. But here's the thing, I always managed to come up with a **better** dough. In fact, an entire selection from our bread line today, was a product of one of those occasions when I had to revive a dead dough.

When we're faced with failures, drowning in problems, under the weight of a mountain of financial debt, or worse, facing a health crisis, we ask ourselves repeatedly. "What have I done that led to this mess?" And I encourage you to continue asking this question. It is not to make you feel more condemned or miserable, but to try to lead you to specific ingredients that you need to add or adjust as you are being remixed by God.

It's pointless to ask God to fix another dough in your life; perhaps your husband, or friends, or business partners or kids. Right now, you are the dough that needs fixing. And the best way for you to find out the answer to this question is through the Word of God. And whatever God leads you to do, big or small, He will surely give you the strength to do it.

When I surrendered myself under God's hands, He revealed to me, almost daily the areas of my character that needed adjustments. He showed me the things that I had done that contributed to our problems. It was during this time that I clung more and more to Jesus being full of "grace and truth". He showed my true self and He guided me with His grace.

Practical Guide:

1. In my 10 years of experience in bread baking, I've never once encountered a dead dough that refused to be revived. On each instance, it just surrendered itself under my skillful manipulation. Tell God *"Lord, I trust You, that You will hold me with your gracious hands during this painful time of remixing. I don't want to stay this way. I'm sorry that I missed the mark. I'm sorry for all my mistakes. I know that You can turn me around. I want to see your ultimate purpose in my life. I want to be useful again. I yield myself to You. You know what to do. I'm all yours."*

2. Read the meditation verse in at least 5 translations and wait for the Holy Spirit to reveal to you His thoughts.

Brace yourself to be remixed to become useful **again**.

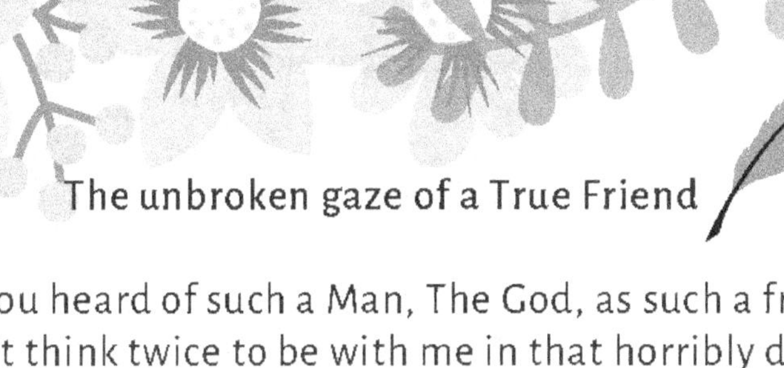

The unbroken gaze of a True Friend

Have you heard of such a Man, The God, as such a friend?
Who didn't think twice to be with me in that horribly dark bend
When all others have said their goodbyes
I had no one else to look at but only His eyes

Have you known anyone who'll always be there?
Who will never let you alone with your burdens to bear
And never minded if you forget about His presence
He knew you'd come back for His love, your Essence

Have you known anyone else who know you so well?
Everything you've ever done, even those you don't dare tell
You know He knows yet He looks at you the same way
Not enough transgressions could take his gaze away

James 1:21-25
New International Version (NIV)

Therefore, get rid of all moral filth and the evil that is so prevalent and humbly accept the word planted in you, which can save you. Do not merely listen to the word, and so deceive yourselves. Do what it says. Anyone who listens to the word but does not do what it says is like someone who looks at his face in a mirror and, after looking at himself, goes away and immediately forgets what he looks like. But whoever looks intently into the perfect law that gives freedom and continues in it—not forgetting what they have heard but doing it—they will be blessed in what they do.

Chapter 20: Let and watch them smile even if you can't

One day I had a strong desire to get out of the house for some fresh air. I got into the car and started driving lazily along the streets of our village. It was one of those days when I felt particularly sad on top of the usual dread and fear. I weaved through the streets very slowly taking time to observe and stare at the house designs, hoping to forget the physical pain in my chest. After a few minutes of driving I reached the village clubhouse. I parked by the pool, lowered down the car windows and turned off the engine. There was a gentle breeze that came through me and calmed my breathing.

Then the sound of laughter started to drift across the lawn, so immediately I started the engine and closed the windows. I had the strong urge to quickly drive out of that place before anybody saw me, but the sudden surge of adrenalin did the opposite and I found myself unable to move though my heart was racing a mile a minute. I was so thankful that the car tint was very dark so the people who started to walk across the lawn couldn't see me.

I peered at them and realized I knew these people. I used to play badminton with them almost daily. They were carrying their badminton gears and they were all sweaty. I watched them as they laughed and joked around and bid each other 'till next time'. They all looked happy and those that weren't laughing were smiling from ear to ear. I realized I was frowning, and these words were playing in my head:" *Why were they smiling? Did they really 'feel' like smiling or were they just pretending?"* I squinted through the sunshine and stared harder at their faces. They looked genuinely happy. One was already at her car door, her friends gone, and yet she was still smiling.

Then I saw myself in their position, several months ago. I was "them" in the past. I was happy and laughing as we finished a badminton game. There was always that unmistakable feeling of satisfaction after profusely sweating or winning a match. However, even as I recalled this, it still didn't make feel "happy".

Being depressed and fearfully anxious made me forget about feeling and being happy and joyful. Seeing the radiant faces of those people I knew, reminded me of being happy; that people could still feel genuinely joyful. **It dawned on me that not because I don't feel it, it doesn't make it untrue**; not because I can't smile doesn't mean people who do aren't sincere when they smile.

Believe it or not, this realization was a big help for me. It brought me a step closer to my recovery. Yes, it didn't make me want to smile. It didn't give me any reason to smile either but hear me. This episode **re-introduced** me to the reality that happiness is **real**; that joy is real and that it can be felt and experienced. I know that I was still a long way to go, but for now I muttered a quiet prayer of thanks to God for this time.

Practical Guide:

1. Don't be afraid to look at "happy" people. Stare at them for as long as you can. Observe their gestures. When I realized I could do this and that I didn't have to be affected while observing them, I actually began to enjoy it.

2. I especially like to observe children of all ages, even those sucking their feeding bottles in their strollers being pushed by their moms in the mall. I would try to imagine how it felt not to have a care in the world; not to feel any worry and to always have that assurance that you're loved and taken care of. I also love the way they observed me when they noticed that I was staring at them. They looked cautiously between me and their parents, quietly waiting for either one of them to notice that their kid was being stared at. I would force myself to smile and that almost always relaxed them. Soon I wasn't "forcing"

it anymore. Soon I was exchanging smiles with the parents themselves.

Let them and watch them smile even if you can't…. **Until you can**.

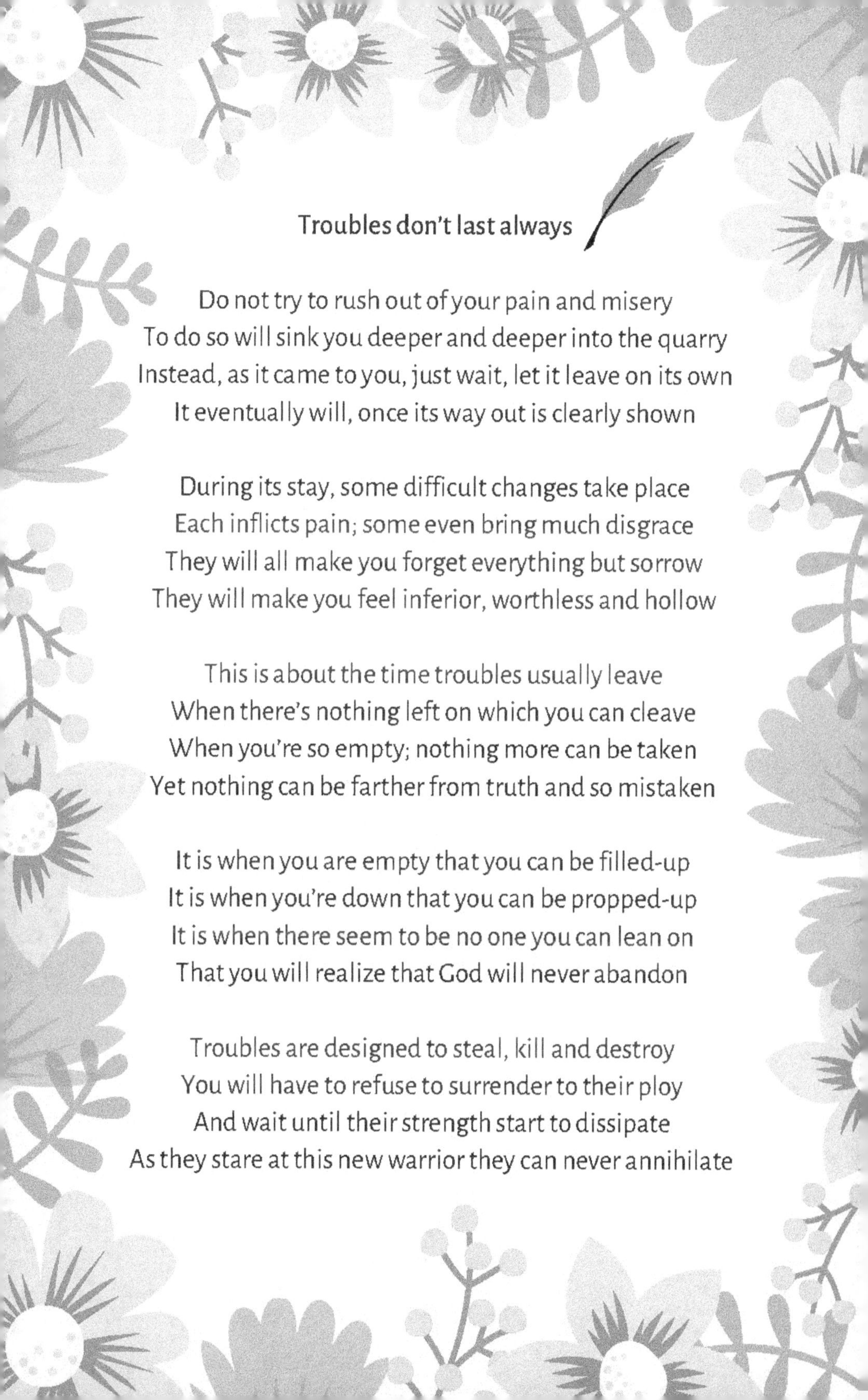

Troubles don't last always

Do not try to rush out of your pain and misery
To do so will sink you deeper and deeper into the quarry
Instead, as it came to you, just wait, let it leave on its own
It eventually will, once its way out is clearly shown

During its stay, some difficult changes take place
Each inflicts pain; some even bring much disgrace
They will all make you forget everything but sorrow
They will make you feel inferior, worthless and hollow

This is about the time troubles usually leave
When there's nothing left on which you can cleave
When you're so empty; nothing more can be taken
Yet nothing can be farther from truth and so mistaken

It is when you are empty that you can be filled-up
It is when you're down that you can be propped-up
It is when there seem to be no one you can lean on
That you will realize that God will never abandon

Troubles are designed to steal, kill and destroy
You will have to refuse to surrender to their ploy
And wait until their strength start to dissipate
As they stare at this new warrior they can never annihilate

Proverbs 15:13
New International Version (NIV)

A happy heart makes the face cheerful,
but heartache crushes the spirit.

Psalm 68:3
New International Version (NIV)

But may the righteous be glad and rejoice before God;
may they be happy and joyful.

Chapter 21: Welcome and embrace the improved you

"The dough that died and lived again"
Part 5

*I*t's really no use resisting God's "remixing". As I told you, I never had a dough "resist" me as a baker. As a result, all dead dough was revived to a higher standard that yielded much better breads than originally planned.

One of those areas that God remixed in me had to do with my temper. During the first few months of my depressed years, I developed a very nasty habit of screaming at my kids whenever they would make a mess. And I mean "scream", at the top of my lungs, banged doors, and threw things that made the most sounds. I didn't hurt them physically, but I knew that I was doing just as much damage to their emotions. And each time I did, I was exhausted, repentant and ashamed of myself.

I asked God to help me. I prayed over and over, *"I don't want to be like this, oh God. My kids deserve better, they need better. I want to be a better example to them. I want them to know grace and mercy through me."* Soon after praying, God started to help me realize that those outbursts coincided with my monthly periods, so I asked God to help me be more "aware" of my moods during those times.

As God made His adjustments with me, I still had occasional breakdown and failures, and the yearning to change grew more. I just wanted to be free from those uncontrolled outbursts and to be aware that I was free, so I started to be really conscious of how I felt during those days (nearing and during my monthly period) and I would tell myself *"This is your hormones talking and feeling Rose, this is not you. You don't have to lose it no matter what reasons you have around you. You can react differently. You can react God's way, or don't react at all."*

The Lord saw my heart, my desire to please Him in this area, and He went to work with me. Today, I am "nearly" free from these urges. I can say I have better control over them and the difficulties during these times of each month hardly manifest themselves at all. And when they do, I almost feel excited to snuff them out.

Just recently, my husband and son were having a heated argument. It was very exasperating, and when I entered our bedroom I felt like banging the door shut. Instead, I closed it, purposely, as softly as I could and breathed deeply and slowly, smiled and whispered, "I'm a new person in Christ."

Practical Guide:

1. Several years after recovering from depression, I researched extensively on its causes. My two sons are now young adults. They're facing so much more challenging experiences, and I wanted to make sure that I helped them avoid falling into the same pit of depression that I did. When you read these materials, you will learn that a deficiency in Niacin or Vitamin B3 is a major cause of depression (including bi-polar) and anxiety:

    a. Reviews of NIACIN: The Real Story
       (http://www.doctoryourself.com/niacinreviews.html)

    b. Vitamin B3 for Depression: Case Report and Review of the Literature
       (https://ionhealth.ca/wp-content/uploads/
       resources/PDFs/Vitamin-B3-for-Depression-Case-
       Report-and-Review-of-the-Literature-25.3.pdf)

    c. Vitamin B3: Deficiency Symptoms
       (http://www.newsmax.com/FastFeatures/health01-
       Vitamin-B3-Deficiency/2011/02/23/id/387137/)

    d.   How to Take Niacin (Vitamin B3) for Depression and Anxiety (https://www.foodmatters.com/article/how-to-take-niacin-vitamin-b3-for-depression-and-anxiety)
Read more about Niacin.

2. Fast-track your recovery from depression by taking mega-doses of Niacin. The ones my whole family take is No-Flush Niacin called Inositol Hexanicotinate. Make sure you take Niacin with Vitamin C.

3. Watch these helpful YouTube videos on the links between Niacin and Depression:
    a.   Nutritional Links to Depression and Mental Illness (https://www.youtube.com/watch?v=HiI7AcH1UIU)
    b.   Dr. Mercola Interviews Dr. Andrew Saul (https://www.youtube.com/watch?v=8ru6IPFPeTQ)

An improved version of you **is coming**. Welcome it and embrace it.

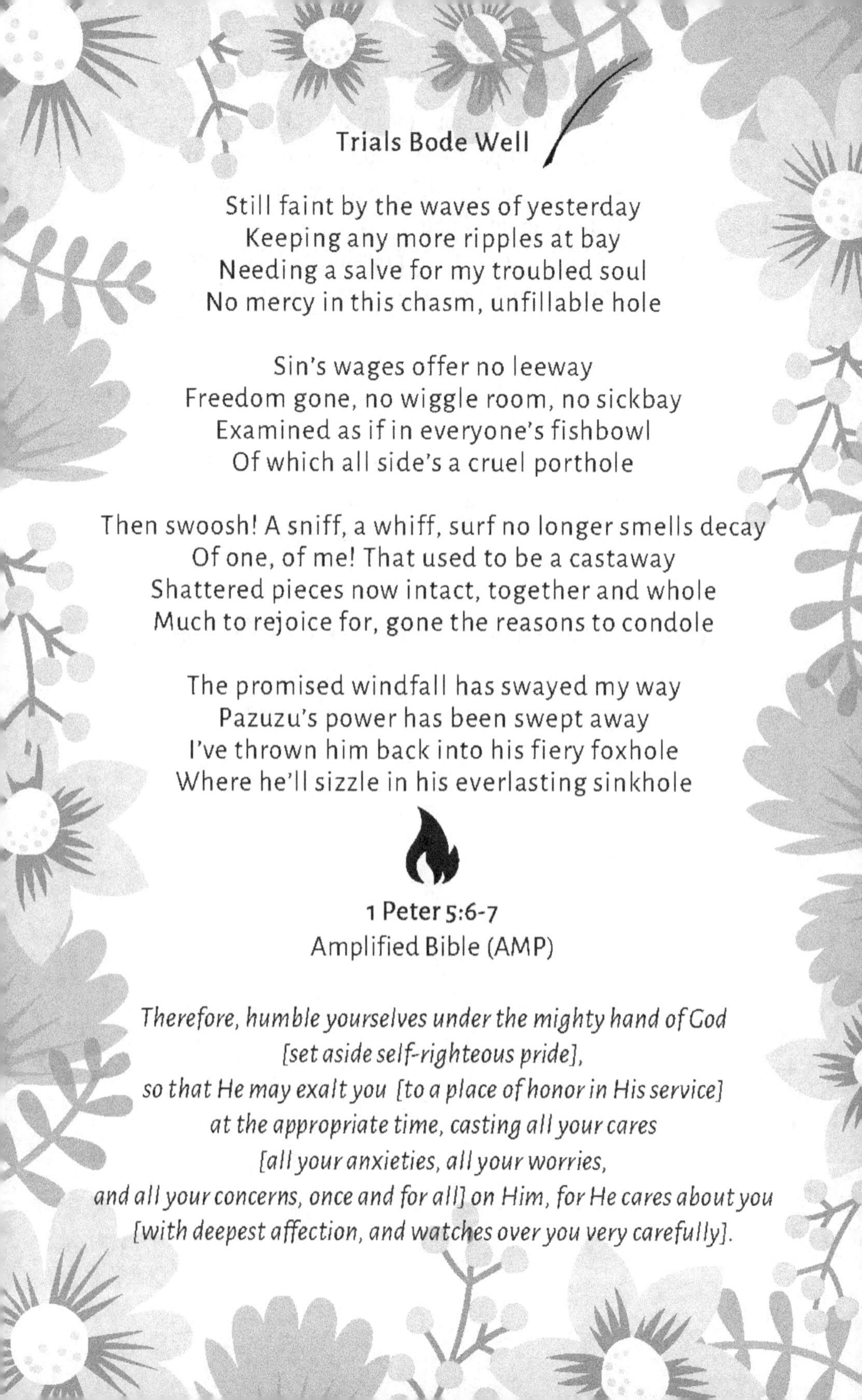

Trials Bode Well

Still faint by the waves of yesterday
Keeping any more ripples at bay
Needing a salve for my troubled soul
No mercy in this chasm, unfillable hole

Sin's wages offer no leeway
Freedom gone, no wiggle room, no sickbay
Examined as if in everyone's fishbowl
Of which all side's a cruel porthole

Then swoosh! A sniff, a whiff, surf no longer smells decay
Of one, of me! That used to be a castaway
Shattered pieces now intact, together and whole
Much to rejoice for, gone the reasons to condole

The promised windfall has swayed my way
Pazuzu's power has been swept away
I've thrown him back into his fiery foxhole
Where he'll sizzle in his everlasting sinkhole

1 Peter 5:6-7
Amplified Bible (AMP)

*Therefore, humble yourselves under the mighty hand of God
[set aside self-righteous pride],
so that He may exalt you [to a place of honor in His service]
at the appropriate time, casting all your cares
[all your anxieties, all your worries,
and all your concerns, once and for all] on Him, for He cares about you
[with deepest affection, and watches over you very carefully].*

Chapter 22: Follow the right pattern

I envy those who can say "I look up to my Mom. I look up to my Dad. He's my hero. If not for my parents, I wouldn't be the person that I am today."

I've always wondered how it was to have a parent whose approval a child always cherished. I never felt that. My father was a womanizer, gambler and an alcoholic. The only positive thing I could think of about him was that I never saw him physically hurt my mother nor verbally abuse her. My mother, on the other hand, was the expressive one. As a young girl, I had lots of memories of her screaming at Papa for coming home late, for having been caught with another woman, or being drunk. Later on, Mama became quieter and a recluse. Many times, I saw her crying, alone in her bed. Even as a young girl, I wished so many times that Mama would decide to leave Papa for good. I resented her for putting up with Papa's womanizing.

About the time I was in my teens, Papa's gambling worsened. Soon Mama took over the management of our tailoring business as Papa became more incapable of keeping it afloat. I witnessed how Mama managed to pay off each of Papa's business and gambling debts until eventually Mama was able to have considerable savings in the bank. Papa learned about this money, so he gambled even more. On many occasions, I saw Mama issuing check payments to settle Papa's gambling debts that he incurred the previous days.

Undeterred, Mama tried investing in real estate. Then the same thing happened: whatever Mama managed to save got burned up by Papa's gambling. This was the time I developed a strong feeling of disgust for Papa. And I felt repulsed by men who exhibited anything similar to what my father did. I also harbored a feeling of contempt towards Mama for tolerating Papa's ways.

But, ironically, after having examined the steps that I took that led to my own family's problems, it was like seeing my father's footsteps. I displayed the same neglect of commitments; the same loose management of financial matters; and the same lack of planning for the future. Despite how I felt toward my father, inadvertently, I followed the same pattern.

Realizing this was a huge step that I took towards the right direction. Admitting to myself this mistake enabled me to see my other options, as good examples to follow. I had siblings, whose lives suddenly opened up to me as worthy patterns to follow. Then I sought constant counsel from my D-group leader. (D-group is short for Discipleship Group, weekly small group gatherings of common church members who live in an area). Also, I derived inspirations from Sunday church messages and during weekdays, I watched Christian TV programs.

However, it was each time I exposed myself to the Word of God that I felt most sure of the direction I was going; that I felt I was following a true road map that would never lead me astray. The Bible became the final and truest design against which I compared all other patterns.

Practical Guide:

1. If you don't have yet, find a Bible-based church that's near where you live. If you have small children, choose a church that offers Sunday school classes for kids whose class time is the same as the service schedule. During my depressed years, my sons were 10 and 13 years old. It was a big burden off my shoulders to see them learn good morals and values through their Sunday school classes. Our church offered these classes per age from ages 3-4 to 15 years old. If you can't find a church that offers Sunday school, then take your kids with you, but make sure that you bring activities they can do by your side quietly. Tablets are great in keeping them occupied, or you may also bring coloring books and crayons. Make sure also that you bring snacks with you for your kids. Remove biscuits from foil

packaging and transfer them in plastic containers or resealable sandwich bags for easy and noiseless access. Explain to your kids why you're doing this and let them learn about the value of being considerate and watch them bring this value all the way to their adulthood.

2. Good patterns and examples can be found everywhere, most especially if you avoid being judgmental of people's mistakes. When you keep an unbiased mind and seeing eyes, you can learn even from the worst of people.

Make sure you are following the right pattern, but always compare it to the **best of all**, the Word of God.

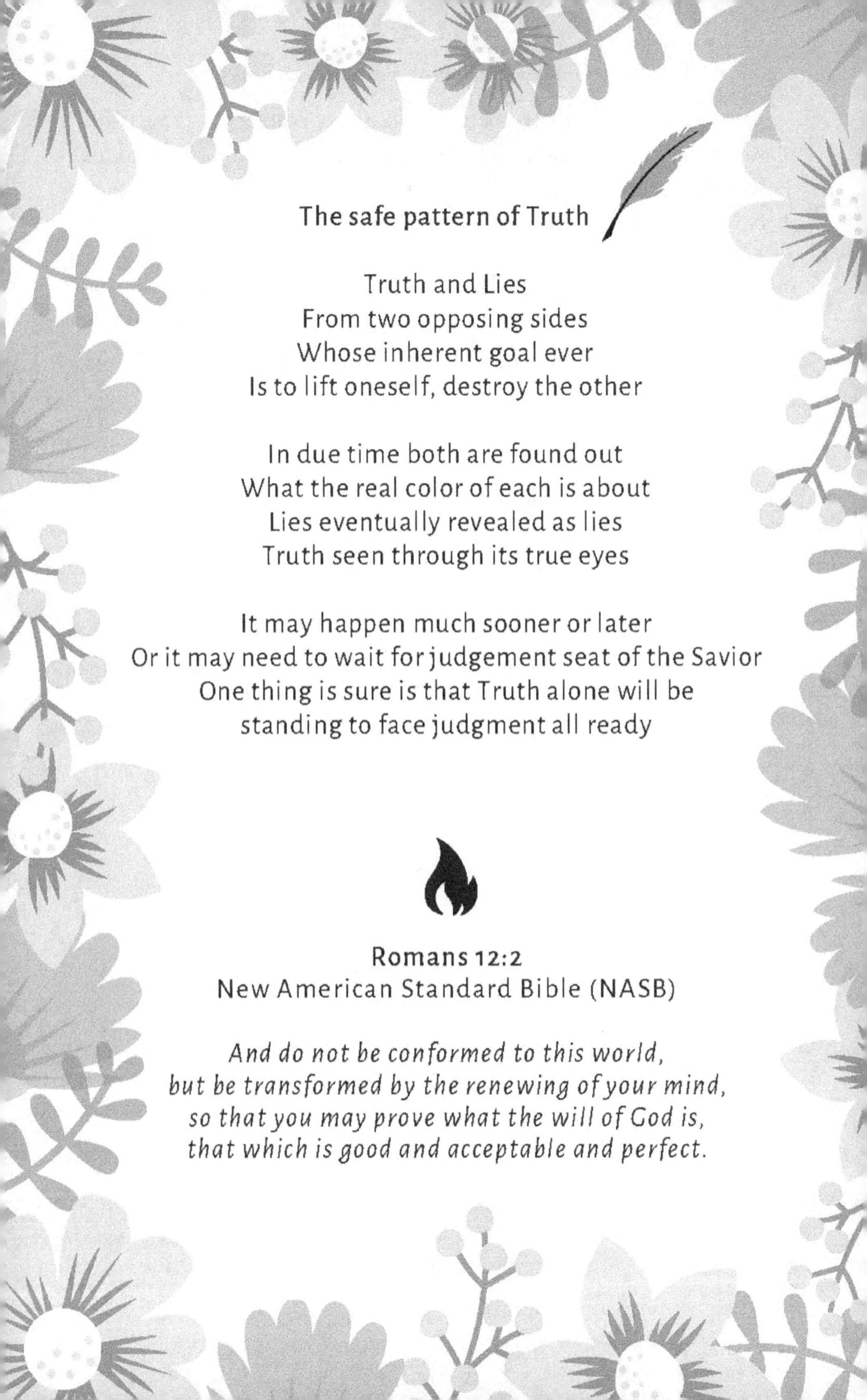

The safe pattern of Truth

Truth and Lies
From two opposing sides
Whose inherent goal ever
Is to lift oneself, destroy the other

In due time both are found out
What the real color of each is about
Lies eventually revealed as lies
Truth seen through its true eyes

It may happen much sooner or later
Or it may need to wait for judgement seat of the Savior
One thing is sure is that Truth alone will be
standing to face judgment all ready

Romans 12:2
New American Standard Bible (NASB)

And do not be conformed to this world,
but be transformed by the renewing of your mind,
so that you may prove what the will of God is,
that which is good and acceptable and perfect.

Chapter 23: Just give in... don't resist

"The dough that died and lived again"
Part 6

God knew that I was in so much pain. God knew exactly how I was feeling. All the dread, the weakness in my joints, the constant fear and feelings of foreboding, my heart's 24/7 palpitations, all my worries and anxieties, and all my problems were not hidden from God. He knew all these and how to help me with them. He didn't know just what to do; He also knew what to do based on what he knew about me. Whatever He had planned for me was for me alone, a unique one.

In the same way, as a baker, reviving a dead dough, I had to put all my attention to that particular dough. I wasn't thinking of the dough the day before, nor another dough in another mixer. My attention was on that particular dough, at that particular time. And everything that I was considering to be able to revive it was for that purpose exactly: to revive the dough, and-not to hurt it further, nor to weaken it.

I tried to figure out everything that I could to be able to help bring it up to a new level. After examining the dough very carefully, I decided on the exact adjustments that I needed to do, certain that it would help in reviving my dead dough. Everything was carefully thought-out. I never just indiscriminately made my adjustment, knowing how it would affect the dough. Almost always I knew the effect or result to expect even before I made it. This was because I knew how the dough would react to my adjustments.

I am so glad that God exercised the same care and thought and even so much more during those three years of my depression. Each time He had to make any sort of adjustments with me, I felt **capable** for the adjustment. I felt strengthened. I felt willing. I knew, without any shadow of doubt, that whatever it was that He was making me do, I was capable of doing it.

However, I'm not saying that I never pulled any tantrums, because I did, a lot! Many times, I kicked and pouted before I did anything. But God was very patient with me.

Practical Guide:

1. Keep minding your gut. Our mental health is closely linked to the health our gut (mostly large intestines). The state of your gut plays a huge role in governing the state of your mind and emotions. It is in the gut where 90% of serotonin is produced (appx 10% only in the brain). When we are under stress, we feel with our senses, including our eyes, and we process with our brain, but it is our gut that determines how we stand under that stress. The more serotonin we have in our gut and the less "leaky" our gut is, the more we are able to withstand even the most intense stress we are under. I provided loads of evidenced-based information on this crucial subject in my first book: *Depression and Intense Anxieties: Your Quickest Way Out*. Here are my recommendations on how you can improve the health of your gut, and subsequently, your mental health:

   a. Eat foods rich in probiotics (such as kimchi, kombucha, raw and unsweetened full fat yoghurt, kefir, fermented tofu, etc.) or take high-quality probiotics supplements.

   b. Eat as much as natural fats as you can: butter, steak, porkchops with thick fatty rinds, eggs, full fat milk, heavy cream, fatty fish like salmon and mackerel, etc. These foods are rich in cholesterol and cholesterol is the vital building component of all our neural cell membranes, our gut wall, and even our neurotransmitters like serotonin and dopamine. Avoid hydrogenated fats and polyunsaturated vegetable oils like canola and corn oil. These are very harmful and inflammatory substances that inflict damage on the lining of our gut which results to leakiness. This leakiness, or intestinal permeability, is what keeps our immune system on a constant overdrive that is manifested through: persistent fatigue, chronic diarrhea or constipation, brain fog, memory loss, headaches, skin conditions, asthma, joint pain, and a host of mental issues like depression and uncontrolled anxieties.

c. Limit your processed sugar intake to bare minimum. Reserve your sugar consumption through moderate consumption of fruits. Processed sugar is both an anti-nutrient and highly inflammatory substance. As part of the diet, processed sugar doesn't do our body any good. At any time, the body needs sugar, it can make it. This is called glucogenesis. Just like its Maker, our body is intelligent. Given the right raw materials, and unhindered by inflammations caused by harmful substances like sugar, it can regenerate itself back to health: physically and mentally.

d. Having some sunshine. 20 minutes anytime from 10 a.m. to 3 p.m., most days of the week, could do wonders for your mood. It doesn't have to be your whole body. A portion, like your legs, tummy or back should be sufficient. Do not put any sun lotion on the area you are to expose. When the complete sun's rays (both UVB and UVA) touch your skin, the cholesterol under your skin goes to work right away. Vitamin D is produced, and this nuclear vitamin goes straight to where it is needed. In a person suffering from depression, this vitamin immediately fires up the production of serotonin in your gut. That is why your body needs to have a constant supply of cholesterol, so that whenever your gut is suffering from low serotonin levels, it can kick itself back into producing this vital happy molecule your mood is dependent on.

2. Keep taking your daily dose of Niacin (Flush-Free) and Vitamin C. I take two 500mg Niacin with two 500mg Vitamin C. If you have stomach acidity, choose the ester or buffered kind of Vitamin C. Or

you may take your regular vitamin C with a buffer like water or some food. Niacin is a precursor in the production of serotonin. The earlier you take these in the day, the better, and the longer stretch of the day you will have feeling positive and anxiety-free.

3. Each time you meditate on the Word and you feel that God is turning some dials here and there as He adjusted you, avoid jumping right into it. Give it time. Let it simmer. God usually is not in a hurry. He is a cool God. He is never short of time. So even if you feel like you're being asked by God to correct a mistake, it doesn't mean that you should have done it yesterday. Ask Him to reveal to you the specific steps you need to take. With me, He always did.

Feel and stay relaxed under God's capable hands. **Just give in**, don't resist.

You Better Mind Gutsy Me

Most of me lives 10 inches below the door
I outnumber you in one way and more
I lay quiet, seemingly by you always ignored
But am I really quiet? Can I remain unhonored?

I was thought to be useless, just a mere menace
How is that? When I am so commonplace
I am everywhere and in everyone
I'll be here long after you're all gone

I don't have eyes, ears, nose or teeth
But you are sure to feel it each time I seethe
All I need are signals and pain is my voice
Shouting when you need to make the right choice

Though tiny but stronger than most
So many of me, unlike you, my singular host
But trillions of an orchestra needs a skillful conductor
You command me, legion in number

Science says I am in-charge of your health
And that I do it in such perfect stealth
But without you in wise and good command
Much of me, though not all, will end up in wasteland

No doubt, you are superior and over me, my tube
Yet I am vital, your life, your fuel, your lube
And don't forget that I simply inhabit you, my passing shell
I may weaken, but as you rot I'll be better and well

It's wise then to make the most of your life
By minding me before sicknesses you are rife
For it is at your own peril and incredible pain
If my health and well-being you would fail to gain

Drink from me

The pain that used to be a constant wraparound
He poured in a chalice and they now astound
Those who drink from it don't ever run aground
Kept safe from the landmines hidden in the ground

Matthew 12:20
New International Version

A bruised reed he will not break,
and a smoldering wick he will not snuff out,
till he has brought justice through to victory.

1 Corinthians 10:13
New American Standard Bible (NASB)

No temptation has overtaken you,
but such as is common to man;
and God is faithful, who will not allow you
to be tempted beyond what you are able,
but with the temptation will provide
the way of escape also,
so that you will be able to endure it.

Chapter 24: Use the ashes to build your new life

"The dough that died and lived again"
Final Part

One day, I was crying and feeling dejected. I was staring at my laptop's screen for several minutes, working on a new batch of bread formulas. At that time, I had just finished test baking the first batch of bread formulas and our bakery was already baking and selling these items, though only in small quantities.

I was feeling hopeless and useless because I wanted so much for our bakery to grow. I wanted it badly to sell hundreds or thousands of breads so that my husband could finally come home. But our sales were moving slower than a snail. I thought *"what is the point of formulating more bread recipes when we couldn't even sell what we have already in volume and big quantities?"*

In my gut instinct, I could feel this strong need to make more bread formulas, but it was being obstructed by what I see. In reality, other than that inner, strong and consistent, almost primal urge to make more formulas and test them, there was no source of encouragement at all. **None.**

God must have seen my despair. He promptly sent two inspirations to keep me going and have kept me going for the last ten years.

The first one happened in a phone call. It was a call from the wife of my husband's coworker overseas. She asked me about the bakery franchise we had bought because she and her husband wanted to put up a business as well. Her husband was feeling homesick and their kids were starting to be more demanding of their father's presence.

I felt so bad that I had no good news to tell her. After recalling from memory, the events that led to our franchised bakery's downfall, I was waiting for her to *say "oh my goodness! I'm sure glad that didn't happen to us!" (this would not have offended me at all because I never would have wished it to happen to anyone)*. But instead, she said *"well, are you willing to sell your bread formulas to me?"*

I was taken aback by what she said and was silent for a long time. For days, I was silent as mixed emotions raged in me.

First, I thought *"Are you kidding me? I've devoted hundreds of hours, thousands of pesos and pails of tears in making these formulas. These are ours and ours only. They're priceless!"*.

Then I thought *"Will they be able to protect these formulas like their own?"*.

Then one day I heard myself ask *"But if I actually do, how much would I sell it for?"*

The second inspiration appeared in a dream. The same one came repeatedly three times on different nights, and on its third time, I woke up with all the details vivid in my mind. In my dream, I was in a room with white walls and white ceiling. There were two to three big men standing on chairs with their hands raised towards the ceiling. They were trying to open some sort of a vault.

I looked intently at the vault on the ceiling and it had three locks. One was a steel wheel similar to those in banks. Another was something that needed to be pulled up and down. The last one required a combination of numbers. Everything was gleaming white. The men on the chairs made their attempts over and over, but the vault failed to open.

When they sensed my presence, I was suddenly standing on a chair, raising my arms up and working with the wheel, the lever and the keypad. The door opened on my first try and as soon as it did, white flour speckled with dusts of gold gushed out of it in steady stream.

Then the scene suddenly changed. This time, I was standing on the floor surrounded with sacks filled with gold-dusted flour and I was filling up more sacks and stacking them against the wall. I saw my face and it looked determined and purposeful, but there was something else. I looked at my heart and I sensed what it was; disappointment.

And as soon as I felt disappointed, I heard the Lord speak to me *"Yes, Rose. You heard me correctly. Those sacks of flour with specks of gold are not for you. They're for other people who need them more. But it's **you** whom I have anointed to bring it to them. **This is your purpose now.**"*

"However, the gold dusts symbolize the bread baking training business that you will put up out of the dust of your former business' collapse. This will be your new and lasting business that will reach many of your countrymen all over the world. The flour that you are putting in sacks symbolizes the bakeries that your future students will put up in answer to their prayers for a business."

The last scene was one where I was ordering people here and there as to how many more sacks to fill up, where to stack them and to whom they should be sent. The oddest thing about it was the location. It was in the house that my mother bought when I was still a young girl, but eventually lost due to my father's gambling. I could even see the open green space at the back of the house where Mama wanted to have a small swimming pool.

Everything in the dream spoke volumes about one thing: restoration; being revived for a purpose.

Soon after I had the dream, God started working with my heart and my unwillingness to share my formulas, even for a fee. The unwillingness was replaced by hesitancy, and my hesitancy was eventually taken over by a firm resolve to be an effective teacher of Filipino breads and bakery management.

As soon as I have set my heart to willingly teach and impart everything that I have learned about breads and bakery management, the puzzle pieces began to fall at exactly their right places. The entire curriculum for the bread baking training started taking shape in my head, and soon I was typing away the words in my laptop.

Six months after God gave me those two inspirations, I posted a free advertisement on the internet. It's a simple ad on a class for anyone who would wish to learn about how to put up their own bakery, breads inventory and bread baking, without the need to purchase an expensive bakery franchise, all for a minimal fee. Two weeks after the advertisement was released, all ten slots were filled up, and a week after the last slot was paid for, I conducted my very first bread baking class.

I had to exercise a great deal of self-control to stop myself from crying while teaching. I couldn't believe where I was then, compared to where I've been just a few months back. In just a very short period, God had started rebuilding everything that was burnt and lost, and He used those ashes as foundation for a new business that will help not just my family, but so many other families as well.

It has been ten years since that very first batch, and I and my husband have taught thousands of overseas Filipino workers who now have their own bakeries.

Every now and then our students would ask *"where and from whom did you learn these bakery principles that you teach us now?"* and I would say with a smile *"from God's School of Experience"*.

And every now and then we would receive messages of thanks from students expressing their gratitude for teaching them the shortest and safest route to having their own bakery business. We have gone through the landmines of bakery business and are now capable of guiding others in avoiding them. This is the purpose of our restoration.

Have you asked God for yours? If you have and you haven't heard His answer, stay at peace, because you're surely on your way to knowing. God may not be early, but He is surely never late either.

Practical Guide:

1. When you feel that you need or should do something, but you don't want to, act like you're ready to do it. Sounds crazy, right? There were many days during those three depressed years that I felt strong enough to do things, but there was always unwillingness, and it was getting the best of me. For example, when I knew that I had to get up from bed and get ready to do some test baking for my formulas, that's exactly what I challenged myself to do: get up from bed. You

would be surprised at how much cobwebs drop off of you just by getting yourself out of bed. It always felt like 50% of the battle had been won already.

It's the same thing I did when I knew that my mind is brewing a new formula, but then I was feeling lazy to face my laptop. I was telling myself "it's not ready yet, it's not ready yet." But each time my fingers touched the keyboard, numbers, formulas and words came out instantly; effortlessly, as if they've been waiting for me to type them and work on them.

2. Right before sleeping at night, think of two to three things you intend to do the following day. For now, just "intend" to do them. That's better than starting the next day without any plans. You would feel better having accomplished one out of two or three goals than doing nothing because you didn't intend to do anything.

3. In the middle of your chaos, be quick to say this to yourself: "God is not done with me. He is still at work and He mean to give me a future and a hope." You can say this even before you get up from bed in the morning. Say it throughout the day and before you sleep at night. It doesn't matter what you feel or whether you believe this or not. Believe me when I say that your heart and mind will soon follow what your mouth declares.

Don't throw the **ashes** away. Use them to build your **new life**, to pave the **new road**.

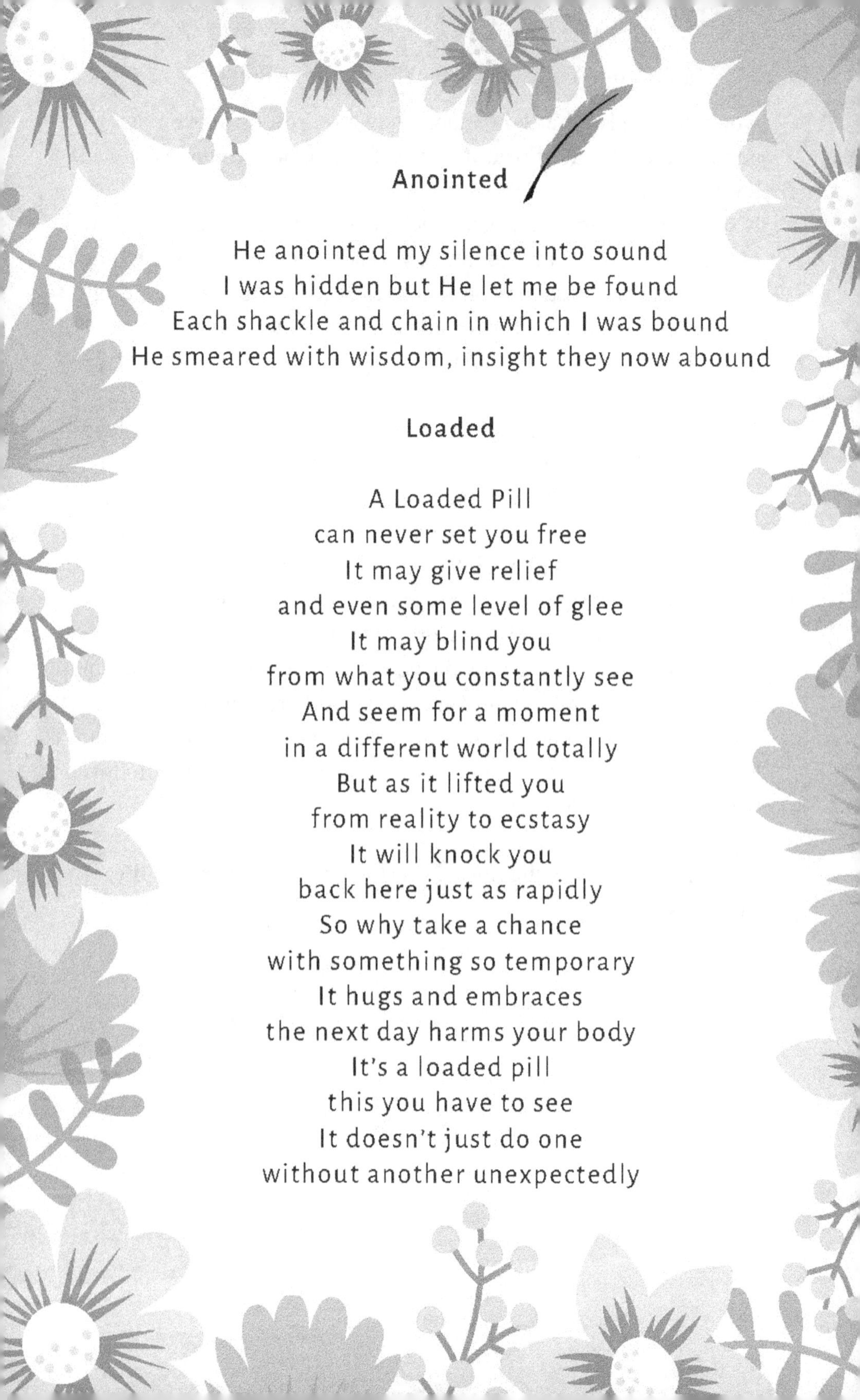

Anointed

He anointed my silence into sound
I was hidden but He let me be found
Each shackle and chain in which I was bound
He smeared with wisdom, insight they now abound

Loaded

A Loaded Pill
can never set you free
It may give relief
and even some level of glee
It may blind you
from what you constantly see
And seem for a moment
in a different world totally
But as it lifted you
from reality to ecstasy
It will knock you
back here just as rapidly
So why take a chance
with something so temporary
It hugs and embraces
the next day harms your body
It's a loaded pill
this you have to see
It doesn't just do one
without another unexpectedly

Forever always over Sometimes

When I found You, I promised to love You forever
Then world showed it could give me much better
That it's fun, delicious, and far much sweeter
So, I thought, maybe "sometimes" is wiser than "forever"

I said, I will be back in a while!
After all I'm Yours for an eternal while
Giddily I hopped and pranced on the colored tile
That led me away from You by his cunning guile

The crafty one said, "This is freedom do you see?
You can act at your will, no boundaries, so carefree!
Enjoy! Doesn't cost anything! That I guarantee!"
Well I got what I liked so I couldn't disagree

Then reds and yellows and pinks turned to gray
The fun and laughter slowly faded away
The noise and then silence don't sound like play
I'm confused! What happens next? Stop the soothsay!

Where is it? The colored tile I used to prance on?
I need to find my way back, please stay, don't abandon!
I feel so alone! Where are you my wily companion?
he replied "I'm right here, making sure with me you stay on"

my heart he gripped in fear, I trembled in terror
Voices, day and night accused me, I needed an Advocator
To plead for my case, stand between me and my aggressor
this crafty one! Oh, I should not have strayed from my Creator!

"My child", He said, "I needed to not stop you
To give you chance to express your freewill too
It grieved Me to see it almost brought you to waterloo
But Love is not Love if you don't willingly choose to do

that which pleases Me, right and worthy
I sent My Only Son to redeem you, nobody forced Me
He, in His own will, chose to die for you and for you to see
that We chose to do so because We loved you so willingly"

My Lord, my Savior, my only True Friend
Forgive me, wash me, I now desire to be with You till the end
I might still make mistakes, digress, go round the bend
but each time I do I ask You to help me comprehend

each misstep, compromise, transgressions in the future
may Your heart I feel and see clearly, not in a blur
just as Yours do, let my heart bleed even before I err
may it burst with pain lest pain to You I render

"My child, I will never tire of helping you know My ways
And even if your promised "sometimes" bring you into dangerous forays
Even there I will be to show you My guiding rays
Because my "Forever" is over your "Sometimes" for always"

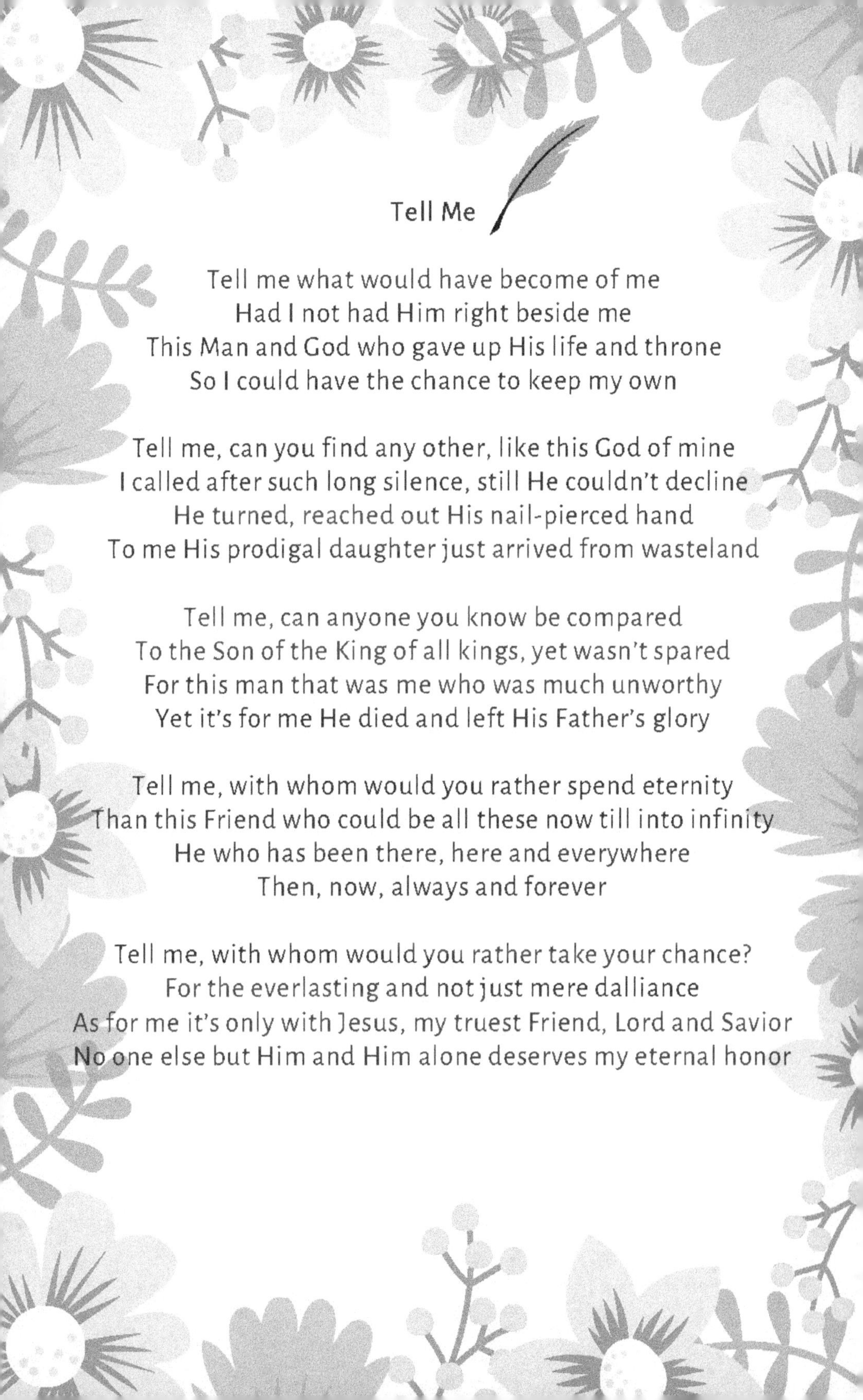

Tell Me

Tell me what would have become of me
Had I not had Him right beside me
This Man and God who gave up His life and throne
So I could have the chance to keep my own

Tell me, can you find any other, like this God of mine
I called after such long silence, still He couldn't decline
He turned, reached out His nail-pierced hand
To me His prodigal daughter just arrived from wasteland

Tell me, can anyone you know be compared
To the Son of the King of all kings, yet wasn't spared
For this man that was me who was much unworthy
Yet it's for me He died and left His Father's glory

Tell me, with whom would you rather spend eternity
Than this Friend who could be all these now till into infinity
He who has been there, here and everywhere
Then, now, always and forever

Tell me, with whom would you rather take your chance?
For the everlasting and not just mere dalliance
As for me it's only with Jesus, my truest Friend, Lord and Savior
No one else but Him and Him alone deserves my eternal honor

Jeremiah 29:11
Amplified Bible (AMP)

For I know the plans and thoughts
that I have for you",
says the Lord,
"plans for peace and well-being
and not for disaster,
to give you a future and a hope.

3 John 2
Living Bible (TLB)

Dear friend,
I am praying that all is well with you
and that your body is as healthy
as I know your soul is.

Conclusion

We are comprised of spirit, soul and body. Whether we believe that our mind and emotions are part of the soul or of the body, it will serve us well to give as much care to our body as we do to our soul and spirit.

Realigning my soul and spirit according to the Word of God (through meditations and honest-to-goodness-pretension-free cognitive and behavioral therapy sessions) made clear the path I ought to be walking on. Now I could see plainly the road ahead and could avoid traps and stumbling blocks. As a result, there were no new problems; the old ones were solved; the debts were getting paid; and broken relationships were being repaired.

Nevertheless, even when the stresses that triggered my depression had subsided, the physical manifestations of my depression kept on: I still couldn't sleep; my body felt weak; my chest continued to pound with palpitations; my hands and feet were constantly sweaty; and the concept of joy and happiness were as distant as they were on Day One of my depression.

As soon as I gave in to my body's cravings for the nutrients that it lacked, only then did those debilitating physical manifestations of depression started to taper off. Hence, as you indulge on this book's generous array of cognitive and behavioral therapy techniques, pay equal attention to the health of your body, particularly your gut.

Here's a quick summary on how you can jump-start your physical healing from depression and intense anxieties:

1. Have regular sunshine: 20 minutes, anytime from 10am to 3pm.
2. Take FLUSH-FREE Niacin (Vitamin B3; Hexanicotinate Inositol is my preferred form of Vit. B3); 2 to 4 capsules daily.
3. Eat cholesterol-rich foods such as raw milk, eggs, heavy cream, salmon, bacon, steaks or any fatty animal meat. Include butter as often as you can in your meals.
4. Eat leafy, green vegetables that are native to your area.
5. Eliminate processed sugar from your diet: sodas and other sugared water, sweet cereals, and sweet snacks.
6. Take bone broth. I prefer beef bones or chicken feet along with other chicken bones.
7. Take supplements: probiotics, Vitamins C, D3, A, B-complex, and K2.

Recently, someone dear to our family, who has been suffering from a severe case of bipolar disorder for the past three years, told me that they are not willing to explore further the nutritional approach to healing their condition. They insisted that putting their mental health in the hands of their medical doctors is still their best option. This person has been in and out of psychiatric clinics and has tried every kind of anti-depressants known today. Despite the absence of any marked improvements, the family still regards these unsuccessful interventions as the only avenue for them.

Their lack of willingness to turn their necks and consider a possible alternative reminded me of how the great Albert Einstein defined "insanity": doing the same thing over and over and expecting different results. This family is one of the inspirations behind the poem "Beyond This" in Chapter 6.

How many times do we need to be proven wrong to realize **we are** wrong? For how much longer do we need to suffer to realize **we are** suffering?

The Do-it-Yourself Therapy Book for Depression

By Rose C. Manalo

Published by Neverbound Publishing House

74 Bel Air Drive, Cor. Fremont St., Laguna Bel Air 1, Don Jose,
Sta. Rosa City, Laguna, Region 4-A, Philippines
Twitter @rosecmanalo1
Instagram @rosecmanalo1
Facebook www.facebook.com/rosecmanalo1
Email rosalinamanalo1970@yahoo.com

Medical Disclaimer:
All information, content, and material in this book is for informational
purposes only and are not intended to serve as a substitute for the
consultation, diagnosis, and/or medical treatment of a qualified physician
or healthcare provider.

Scriptures marked AMP are taken from the AMPLIFIED BIBLE (AMP):
Scripture taken from the AMPLIFIED® BIBLE, Copyright © 1954,
1958, 1962, 1964, 1965, 1987 by the Lockman Foundation Used by
Permission. (www.Lockman.org)

Medical Disclaimer:
All information, content, and material in this book is for informational purposes only and are not intended to serve as a substitute for the consultation, diagnosis, and/or medical treatment of a qualified physician or healthcare provider.

ISBN
Softbound/Paperback: 978-621-8153-08-0
Hardbound: 978-621-8153-07-3
E-Book: 978-621-8153-11-0

121